D0989373

THE NEOTENIC QUEEN

Tales of Sex and Survival in the Sonoran Desert

BY ALEJANDRO CANELOS

Illustrations by Rachel Ivanyi

Tucson, Arizona | 2022

The Neotenic Queen: Tales of Sex and Survival in the Sonoran Desert
by Alejandro Canelos

Published by Neotenic Press

www.neotenicqueen.com

Copyright © 2022 Alejandro N. Canelos

All rights reserved. No portion of this book may be reproduced in any form without permission from the publisher, except as permitted by U.S. copyright law.

Cover Art: "Mother and Father" by Rachel Ivanyi

Illustrations by Rachel Ivanyi

Book design by Gabriela Fleming

ISBN: 979-8-9856789-1-8 (paperback)

To the animals and plants in our backyard

THE CONTENTS

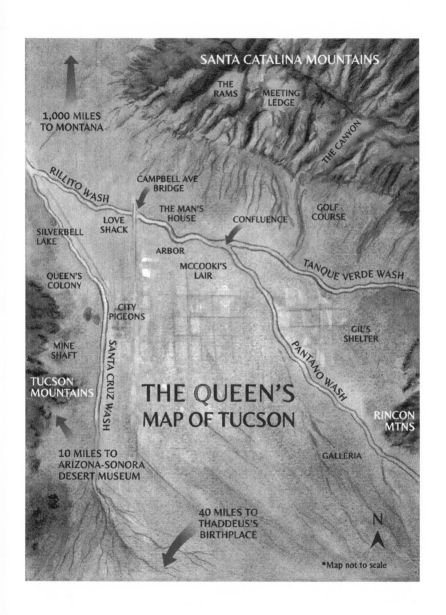

THE QUEEN'S MAP OF TUCSON

SANTA CATALINA MOUNTAINS

THE RAMS

MEETING LEDGE

THE CANYON

1,000 MILES TO MONTANA

RILLITO WASH

CAMPBELL AVE BRIDGE

THE MAN'S HOUSE

LOVE SHACK

CONFLUENCE

GOLF COURSE

SILVERBELL LAKE

ARBOR

MCCOOKI'S LAIR

TANQUE VERDE WASH

QUEEN'S COLONY

CITY PIGEONS

SANTA CRUZ WASH

GIL'S SHELTER

MINE SHAFT

PANTANO WASH

TUCSON MOUNTAINS

RINCON MTNS

10 MILES TO ARIZONA-SONORA DESERT MUSEUM

GALLERIA

40 MILES TO THADDEUS'S BIRTHPLACE

N

*Map not to scale

A VIEW FROM BELOW

The sun was starting up when Jake peered out. The burrow was close to the house, but not too close. If the man came with the shovel, Jake would have time to get away. A displaced ground squirrel glared from across the yard, angry but alive.

The door opened. The man's summertime ritual was to sit outdoors as the sun rose, drinking from a mug. Jake crept out farther, wanting to be seen, but careful not to shake his rattle. The man looked up and down like he was trying to comprehend the dead pack rat at his feet.

Jake said a prayer and came out all the way. He raised his head, moving it in small circles to get the man's attention. Their eyes met, and for a few seconds, Jake thought there was a connection. The man ran inside, and Jake turned around. He knew what was coming.

By the time the man returned, Jake was gone. That he'd failed in his first attempt at communication neither surprised nor discouraged him. Overcoming thousands of years of biological and cultural programming wasn't going to be easy.

Jake was already lucky, one of only three (out of fifteen) who'd survived the first year. A competent hunter, he'd developed a reputation for getting out of trouble. His brother, Adler, thought otherwise. "The kid is dangerous. Too many weird ideas."

At two and a half, Jake had decided to climb a mesquite tree, "To get a better view."

"View of what?" they'd asked.

"That's what I want to know."

He'd dropped to the ground at the last second, eluding the talons of a hawk.

"What did you see?"

He'd refused to tell and, though pressed, stayed silent on the matter.

Six months later, in the fall, he'd broken both fangs trying to puncture an irrigation line. "I was thirsty."

A good idea, except he'd chosen the wrong type of conduit. And while his kin would've hidden in shame, Jake made light of his temporary condition. "I look like a constrictor, and just in time for Halloween!"

He'd have tried again when his fangs came back, but by then he'd become enchanted with a bigger idea: making peace with the man, who'd been endeavoring to rid his garage of pack rats for months, with little success. For every rat the man electrocuted, strangled, bludgeoned, or drowned, two more took its place. They weren't afraid of Jake, either. "Go ahead. Kill us. Eat us. Whatever. Fuck you."

There, in the rats, was where Jake had seen opportunity.

He killed another the next night, making it as painless as possible (the rat deserved less), and laid out the corpse in a spread-eagle position. This time the man tried sneaking around behind Jake, but Jake had anticipated the maneuver and escaped with ease.

Jake's sister, Piper, in general tolerant of his oddities, begged him to reconsider. "Don't do it, little bro. Please."

"Open your mind."

"You're making a mistake."

"Sorry, Pipe. I gotta do this."

"Why? Really, why?"

"The hate. That's why."

"But you're one of the most feared creatures on earth! A God-damned rattlesnake!"

He'd never heard her curse. (It was frowned upon.) He slithered off. Piper meant well, but didn't understand his views. Then again, nobody did.

She called after him. "You're gonna get the shovel!"

He looked back. "You might be right, Sis. But you might be wrong, too."

On his fifth try, something different happened. Instead of grabbing the shovel, now right beside the door, the man sat at the table, never taking his eyes off Jake. They looked at each other for a long time. Whole minutes. Jake moved his head in small circles. The man sipped his drink. Jake was impressed at the man's ability to match stares with a snake.

The man finished his coffee, bagged up the rat carcass, and went inside, without a glance at the shovel. Jake was thrilled.

"Pipe, it's working!"

"Don't tell me that. Adler says you're going to ruin it for everybody."

"Adler's full of ants."

Jake would've preferred a close relationship with his brother, but by the time they'd turned four, they hadn't spoken since the previous brumation.[1] It wasn't worth dwelling on, especially now.

After depopulating the rats from the garage, Jake moved on to a nest behind where the man cooked his food. The man didn't seem to know it was there, even though it was like a condo complex, teeming with foulmouthed rodents.

Over the next few weeks, Jake cleaned it out. The rats sneered and taunted, spewing vulgarities like "dicknose," "shitbag," and "cold-blooded bitch," but they had no way to back up their talk. Each morning, Jake ventured farther from his den, and the man stayed seated. It was a Friday in July when Jake came all the way onto the porch. The man didn't move. He was calm, talking. Talking to a rattlesnake! Jake didn't get the words, but he understood the delivery and body language. Not hate, not fear. Could it be gratitude? The shovel no longer leaned against the house,

---

1   hibernation for cold-blooded animals

having been put away days earlier. The man went inside, leaving the door open, and Jake faced a decision: Run? Or not?

Staying was worth the risk. He moved his head in circles, held his tail still, and prayed.

The man came out with a bowl and placed it on the pavers, then backed in and closed the door. Jake approached and peeked over the edge. Water! The man had given him a bowl of water! He rushed to tell Piper.

"Can you believe it? I'll—I mean, we'll—never be thirsty again!"

"You can't let Adler know," she said. "Promise."

"You're kidding, right? He's going to find out. It's huge news."

"And that's what this is about, isn't it? Your need for glory."

Jake gave up. "Yep, that's it. Glory. I'll see you later, I've got work to do."

Piper was sad, watching him go.

The man emerged at dawn with the shovel. He nodded at Jake as if to say, "This isn't for you," and set about filling several of the larger squirrel holes. It was perfect timing, as Jake had run out of pack rats for the daily offering. The rats would be back, he knew, nastier and more destructive than ever, but in the meantime, the man might like some other help.

The squirrels didn't appreciate it. "We know you need to eat, but how can you kill for *him*? We vermin need to stick together." A reasonable-sounding argument, but Jake's fellowship with the man confirmed what he'd believed all along—that he *wasn't* vermin. And it felt awesome.

Burrows were appearing with less frequency, and the man seemed content. Jake was content too. They couldn't communicate, but their bond was undeniable. After a big drink, Jake had lain down for a nap at the man's feet when he heard a noise. A low hiss. Nearby? He raised

his head. Adler! His brother was creeping along the side of the house, behind the man.

Jake whispered, "What are you doing here?"

"Something I should've done a long time ago, Brother."

"What are you saying?"

Adler didn't respond, now only two lengths away. Not wanting to shake his tail, Jake coiled. The man noticed, but still didn't see Adler, who'd also coiled. The man was about to get bitten! Adler struck, and Jake struck a split second later, meeting Adler in midair and knocking him to the ground.

The man disappeared inside. Adler said, "To Hell with you!"

Jake felt a sting on his flank. In the collision he'd been pierced by one of Adler's fangs. "Why are you doing this? What did the man do to you?"

They faced one another, poised to strike. Their tails swished dozens of times per second with the din of a hundred maracas. Adler said, "I'm here as savior. You've gone against God and nature."

Jake fought off drowsiness. "Leave now. This is your last warning." His muscles began to stiffen.

The man came out with the shovel. He looked at the two snakes hissing and rattling.

Adler said, "See? He can't tell us apart. We're no different after all."

Jake stopped hissing, silenced his tail, and moved his snout in small circles.

Adler's head was separated from his body mid-sentence. His mouth kept going, but the words were slurred, unintelligible.

Jake's eyes turned from slits to marbles before he lost consciousness.

He woke up next to Piper. "Where am I?"

"Safe," she said.

"What about the man?"

"He's fine, but he killed Adler."

"It was Adler's fault."

Piper was quiet for a long time. "You're going to be okay," she said.

"I know."

They lay together, breathing.

Piper spoke. "You never said what you saw from that tree."

"I know."

"Can you tell me? What was it, Jake?"

"I saw rooftops. Lots of them."

"Oh," she said, and watched him drift back into sleep. ♦

CASEY AND CALYPSA

Even in the pinholes of first light, the web was more beautiful than he'd imagined.

He called up. "Hello?"

"Who's there?"

"My name's Casey."

He'd spent half the night traveling to the crawlspace under the abandoned mobile home and trying to find Calypsa's corner, in pitch dark, among hordes of frantic males.

"Not interested. Try Sheila a few spots over."

"That's not why I'm here."

"Why then?"

"Your web. It's magnificent."

A spider three times Casey's size came into partial view.

"Calypsa?" His voice cracked.

"Tell me what you want."

"I was...um...hoping for a tour."

"That's what they all say. Get lost."

"No, really. Your art is what brought me here."

She leaned farther over the ledge, and he saw her abdomen. What he'd heard was true—where the hourglass should've been was solid black.

"You must've been passing by," she said.

He rocked back and forth on his hind legs. "Actually, no. I followed a long silk road with some other guys."

"And where are they?"

"Trying to score. Like everyone else."

"Except you."

"Right."

"Right. Have a nice life." She turned away.

"Wait...please."

"What."

"I meant what I said. The originality, the precision. I'd love to see more of your work."

She glared, and her jaws came out the tiniest bit. "If you're just trying to get into my epigynum,[1] you'll be sorry."

"I swear on my mother's egg sac."

"I'll hang you out for the mud daubers."[2]

"Understood."

"Come up, then. And don't touch anything."

"I won't. I promise."

Casey climbed through a forest of multihued verticals and crept onto the tangle, a dense layer of crisscrossing strands. "Your interior scheme is...a natural look." Her belly was right at his eye level. Not staring took effort.

"White, sand, and cream, in subtle variations. A big change from the triadic harmonies. I haven't decided how I feel about it yet."

"Your vision is extraordinary."

"Thank you." She turned and gestured for him to follow. "My studio is the top floor, anchor to anchor."

They went up to a wide space bordered by modernist landscapes and still lifes on octagonal canvases.

She studied his reaction. "Have a look around, then you'd better run along, if you want any chance at dipping your tips. It might be too late already."

---

1 pronounced with a soft ‹g› as in vagina, with the accent on the second syllable

2 parasitic wasps

"Like I said, that's not why I'm here." He held both pedipalps[3] out straight. "See, they're not even damp."

"You didn't come all this way to see my paintings. Or my web."

"You're right, I didn't."

Her jaws protruded. "I told you..."

"I want you to paint *me*."

"Beg your pardon?"

"I said, I want you to paint me..." He pointed at the underside of his own abdomen. "Here."

She was silent. Her fangs returned to their sheath.

"I want an hourglass. A red one. As big and bright as you can make it."

"You're serious."

"I thought you'd understand."

"What made you think that?"

"You painted over yours."

"That's none of your business."

"Of course, I'm sorry." They stared at each other for a long time. "So...will you?"

The day before, Tim had told Casey he'd never been to the Love Shack either. "But Rick says it's *the shit*. So jammed with horny babes you can smell the hourglass from here, when the wind is right. And birds can't get in."

Casey said, "Rick's been before?"

"No. But he knows all about it."

"Calypsa lives there, right?"

Tim made a face. "What do you want with that weirdo? Get anywhere near her, she'll eat you. I heard."

---

3   spider "arms" that are additional to the eight legs

"Her web is legendary. I'd like to see it before I die."

"Why?"

"I mean, if I'm there already."

"Whatever floats your carapace,[4] man. Anyway, Rick found a trail, so me and him and his brother Larry are going *tonight*." He rubbed his claws together. "I gotta go get ready. Meet back here if you want in."

Larry didn't survive the fifty-yard journey. Last in the caravan, he was picked off around halfway by a praying mantis in a privet.

"My bro wasn't getting any action regardless," said Rick. "He laid a weak rap and couldn't dance."

Tim said, "Still, it's a major bummer when you're this close."

Rick said, "Yeah, so shut up and keep moving."

When they arrived, Rick took a big sniff and flexed his forelegs. "Bitchin! See you losers later." He rushed through a crack in the stairs.

Tim said, "Time to get lucky," and followed.

Casey hesitated. What would she say, when they met? It didn't matter. He was committed.

"Lean farther. You won't fall," said Calypsa.

Casey found a comfortable position. "How's this?"

"Good."

"By the way, where do you get your paint?"

She sat back. "Nobody's ever asked that. Let's see, greens from June bugs and caterpillars, purples from potato bugs and crickets, browns from roaches, grasshoppers, and moths. Oh, and moths are great for yellows too. Blues are rare, so I hardly use them. Black and gray are literally everywhere, and reds...for you, it'll be mostly deer tick."

"Sounds wonderful."

"It is. There's nothing like mammal blood for richness in tone."

---

4   the hard shell covering the top of a spider's midsection

"I'm so lucky to be in your claws."

"I'll do my best. Now don't move, unless you want a pear shape instead."

When she was done, Calypsa pulled a foil gum wrapper from behind an embroidered curtain. "Take a look."

Casey stood over it, studying. "I love it, love it, love it!" He sighed. "It feels so...*right*."

"I'm glad. Don't touch it for half a day."

He thanked her fifteen different ways before he managed to step away from the reflection.

"What will you do next?" she said.

"Build a little web, I guess. Hang out and be me. Enjoy the time I have left."

"You know, there *is* one very small thing you could do for me. If you wanted."

"Anything, Calypsa."

Tim and Rick had struck out all night (they didn't come close) and were looking for a place to rest. Tim said, "Hey, check *her* out."

Rick looked up. "That's a dude."

"Huh, yeah. Why's a dude...?" He went closer. "Hold on... isn't that...?"

Rick said, "No way..."

"It is!" said Tim. "Casey! Yo, Casey!"

Casey was dangling faceup. He pretended not to hear.

Rick said, "Casey scored! How the hell?"

Casey kept still, hoping they'd leave.

Tim said, "Who's the girl? And where'd she go? Morning munchies?"

Rick said, "You musta really rocked her, man!"

They poked each other in the pedicel[5] and laughed.

Casey had no choice. "Yeah, she's off somewhere, not really sure. I'll catch up with you guys later, okay?"

Rick came up the wall with Tim behind, and Casey froze. Should he go up or down?

Too late: Rick had seen. "What is *that*?"

Tim saw right after. "Holy wasps, man. What'd you do?"

Casey said, "Leave me alone, okay?"

Rick said, "Uh-uh, I need a closer look." He lowered himself on his own line until he hovered next to Casey. "If I didn't see it myself, I wouldn't believe it. Dude's got an hourglass."

Tim was on Casey's other side. "I'm looking at it, and I still don't believe it."

Rick stuck out a foreleg. Casey said, "Don't! Leave me alone!"

Rick looked at Tim. "Grab his legs."

They held Casey while Rick poked at the image. Casey tried to wriggle free. "Stop! You're ruining it!"

Rick was laughing, scraping off the red, when Tim said, "Oh no."

Two of Casey's legs had become detached. The remaining ones curled inward, his pedipalps retracted, and pale blue liquid oozed from the holes in his thorax. With his last breath, he said, "Why?"

They left the body dangling and floated to the ground, where Rick wiped his tarsus off in the dirt. "Forget about him. Rest up, man, to-night's gonna be a brand-new ballgame."

"Why wait?"

Rick looked around. "Who said that?"

Calypsa came out from behind a brick. She towered over them.

Tim staggered backward, tripping over his hind legs. "You're... you're that artist."

---

5 waist

"How'd you figure that out?"

He pointed at her abdomen.

"Maybe I've been saving myself." She used a single claw to peel away a strip of paint, revealing brilliant red underneath.

Rick said, "*That's* what I'm talkin' about."

"Come with me." She looked up at Casey's lifeless form. "And bring him. We'll be hungry after." She turned and started walking.

Rick scrambled up to cut the line, and the corpse fell. Tim said, "You sure about this?"

Rick dropped down. "Are you joking? It's exactly what we came for. Now help me."

They dumped Casey in the center of Calypsa's studio. Tim looked around. Something about the artwork made him want to check for exits.

Rick began to shimmy. First his forelegs, then his thorax, then his whole body. "You ready for me, girl? I bet you are."

Tim couldn't help himself and shimmied also. Calypsa tucked her abdomen under and forward, exposing her spinnerets. Rick said, "Yeah, baby, yea...!"

A fibrous missile plastered both of them against an anchor. Within seconds, Calypsa had strapped them to the web and each other.

"Wha...what are you doing?" said Tim.

Rick said, "Can we talk about this?"

She stuffed a ball of sticky thread in each one's mouth. "No, *we* can't."

She held up a small, woven sac. "Do you know what this is?"

They knew.

"Something my friend Casey left behind." She dipped a foreleg. It came out glistening. "Watch closely now." She tucked the leg inside herself.

Rick and Tim tried to get free.

"You'll be well fed with his carcass. Force-fed, if need be. He wouldn't mind at all, under the circumstances."

She watched them struggle. "Until my eggs hatch, twenty days from now. Then, there'll be hundreds of tiny widows wanting fresh, live protein."

She took a dab of black from a hanging palette and re-covered the red on her tummy. "What do you think?"

All eight of Rick's eyes rolled back in his head. Tim passed out.

Calypsa wrapped Casey's body in her finest silk before going to work on the portrait she'd begun earlier that morning. It was for the children. ♦

HUM, HUM, HUM

Crazy burners[1] never rest. I get it, they're only here a few days. I roll over to grab more z's, but can't, 'cause this morning's noisier than usual, and now one of 'em is hovering right over me, talking about a body. What kinda body, I ask. A dead one, she says. She's an Anna's, a looker, and I can see she's scared out of her little hummingbird mind.[2]

Be there in a sec, I tell her. The West End, she says, and buzzes off. The West End, aka the Wild Side, where the hardest partying goes down, all night long, and that's why I sleep as far away as possible, but now it's time to do what I get paid for.

Takes me nine seconds to run the length of the arbor.[3] Not bad for a roadrunner my age.

I don't need to ask where to look, cause there's ten burners clustered at the ceiling. Move, I say. The group scatters when they see me, and there it is: a Broadbill, male, tangled up in the branches. No question he's deceased, and the way things look, it wasn't his idea. I need a better view, so I step out from under the arch and take a running leap to get on top. I almost don't make it, and realize I better get back on my old exercise routine, the one I couldn't keep up after Suzy left.

Being up here's a good reminder of why the resort is so popular with burners: the vines're crawling with protein—ants, grasshoppers, flies, moths, caterpillars, all the good stuff. My job, part of it anyway, is

---

1 hummingbirds
2 The Anna's hummingbird is one of the four most common species in Southern Arizona, along with the Broad-billed, Black-chinned, and Costa's hummingbirds.
3 two dozen grape vines planted in a single row and trained over a curved lattice to create a leafy, branchy "tunnel" 240 feet long

keeping out the nasties—tarantulas, mantises, snakes, frogs, lizards, and whatever other land runners might pose a threat to the burners, who say they can't *really* let loose if they're looking over their shoulder. Makes sense. Anyway, things were going fine, nothing besides a few bumps and scrapes, but now there's a dead one, and they're all looking at me.

I ask a few questions and nobody knows anything, except the same Anna's who woke me heard it was a mantis, that's why she's so shook up. Okay, I think, for argument's sake, if it was, why's anything left? To a mantis, these little birds're nutrition, like they'd be to me, if I wasn't hired to protect 'em. Plus, mantises sleep at night, they're civilized that way at least, so I can't see one climbing all this way in the dark to kill a burner and just leave him. No way.

I take the vic in my beak and the rest clear out. They don't like the visual, but what else can I do? Gotta get back to my office, where I can think. Two months in, seems like the job can't get any cushier, but now there's this, and I better get it sorted out, 'cause if even one burner cancels a reservation, it'll be curtains. El Big Mariachi, aka Big M, aka the property owner and a human and *my boss*, won't have any use for me if I can't keep his resort at full capacity.[4]

First I check with Carlos, who works for Big M too, running security on the larger area, everything outside the arbor. It's open space, with no trees or shrubs anywhere except the West End, so Carlos can patrol the whole thing himself, day and night. You might ask, like I did, was it the job that brought him here, all the way from Montana? Turns out he was running from something back home and this gig dropped in his lap. He hasn't offered the deets, and I won't push, but I am curious if all the coyotes up there have ears as big as his. Another strange thing, he hardly

---

4   What Curtis the roadrunner doesn't know: Big M built an arbor in his backyard for various reasons and later found out, to his delight, that it attracts hummingbirds.

says a word, so different from the local coys, who'll talk your ear off, right up to when they bite your head off.

Any place overflowing with bugs and burners so near town is gonna attract lots of attention. House cats'd have a jamboree, for example, especially at night, but that's where Carlos comes in. Lucky dog must get a dozen cats a month by letting 'em think they can make it to the arbor, and he's lying in wait, and bam! Bye-bye, kitty. Kinda feels like he's using the burners—and me—as bait, but it works. Anyway, it's not my call, 'cause Big M pays the bills, and he makes *all* the calls.

I got no witnesses and no leads, so it's best if Big M doesn't find out yet. The easiest thing'd be to eat the evidence, but I don't want the burners *too* scared of me, especially now. When I first showed up, they couldn't understand why one of their few natural predators was in charge of onsite policing for their all-inclusive, adults only, almost-anything-goes resort, but if you think, it makes perfect sense. I keep order *because* they're afraid of me, and word's gotten around: come party here, 'cause there's a world-class athlete with razor talons keeping you safe. Backed up by a coyote, who's backed up by other coyotes, part-timers, in case a bobcat comes through. (And if it's a puma, everybody can forget it, but good thing, there's none of 'em around, and anyone who tells you otherwise is a liar.) I also let the burners call me *Cuck*, short for cuckoo,[5] which they think is hilarious, and I might too, 'cause of how they say it, all clipped and squeaky, except for what went down with me and Suzy.

I throw the stiff through the fence for Carlos, who gulps it down like nothing, and now he's an accomplice, so hopefully he won't say anything, which feels like a step in the right direction. I tell the burners not to worry, everything's under control. They believe me, and by lunch they're back to their usual wickedness, so I spend the afternoon on another of my regular duties, checking for nests.

---

5 Roadrunners are part of the cuckoo family.

What almost-anything-goes means, basically, is: Don't make a chick. Not that the guests feel restricted—the things I've seen these birds do to each other with their long curvy beaks could peel the bark off a cottonwood. Like one time, an Anna's came up to me (I'm kinda partial to those, can you tell?) claiming she could pull a raisin through a reed with her tongue, and did I wanna see? Only time I ever been hit on by a burner, and honest, I was interested, they run so hot, but I knew Big M woulda been totally opposed, and anyway, the tiny temptress was gone the next day. I mighta dodged a bullet there.

Speaking of raisins, they're a key to the whole operation, as important as water, 'cause when the grapes sit and shrivel, that's what brings the bugs. You might ask the obvious, why don't the doves eat the grapes? Before they dry out? 'Cause the hawks and eagles're on Big M's payroll too. The arbor's so out in the open, any dove tries to land gets carried off by one of the raptors, who sit and watch all day from the tall trees on the edges. At night the owls move in, just in case Carlos and his gang need any help, which I'm betting they don't.

Bottom line, the burners *just love it.* Protected from above by the vines, protected from below by Carlos and me, they party from check-in to check-out like it's 1999, and there's no judgment, 'cause everybody's here for the same thing. As long as they don't make babies—anyone caught breaking *that* rule gets booted for life. Big M had a vision, a safe place for burners to have their freaky fun with no strings attached, and so far, it's been a smash hit. How do I know? A three-day, two-night stay has to get booked over a year in advance. Oh yeah.

I decide to call it an accident and pretend like nothing happened. Next morning though, same thing, a burner's in my face, a big Costa's, and it's still dark out. I get a lump in my throat when he tells me there's another. Another body, you mean? Yeah, he says, near yesterday's.

Uh-oh.

Just off the West End is a pomegranate orchard full of flowers, meaning nectar, aka crystal methamphetamine, aka sugar. Everyone knows how much burners love sugar, but it's not allowed in the arbor, 'cause if it was, there'd be eggs all over, and I'd be taking apart nests as fast as I could find 'em. Meanwhile, Big M has to know I can't stop every guest who wants to sneak off at night for a fix, so he *wants* me to look the other way, right? If he didn't, why'd he plant the pomegranates in the first place? And it's the perfect setup, 'cause the other thing burners love is breaking the rules, as long as there's no enforcement. Makes 'em feel like they're actually doing something, taking a risk.

Well, as it turns out, they are. This time it's a dame, Black-chinned. I'm thinking about how yesterday's vic was in the vine farthest west, and today's is in the next one over, and it's a trend I don't like.

Poor thing's wings're spread out like a crucifixion, and worse, her mouth is glued shut. Now that's a really twisted thing to do to a burner, 'cause if they can't go into torpor[6] fast enough, the life is starved right out of 'em. Is that what happened, or did the perp kill her first and then do it, to send a message? I don't know which is worse.

The burners're panicked, popping around like jumping spiders, and I hafta scare 'em a little to get 'em to settle down. *What's going on*, they all wanna know. Is a killer on the loose? Is it safe to be here? When they start talking about leaving early, I realize: I need to get this sorted out *right now*. It's murder, no joke, and I'm already worried about tomorrow.

Calm down, I say to myself, take a breath. All it was, a couple burners stuck their tongues where they didn't belong, and things went sour. Was bound to happen, and I oughta be surprised it took 'til now. What it means is, tonight I gotta stay in the West End, keep 'em all on the premises. I think about bringing the tumbleweed crown I made for Suzy when

---

6 hummingbird deep sleep with lowered metabolism, heart rate, and body temperature

we got together 'cause it helps me fall asleep, but who am I kidding, I'm pulling an all-nighter anyway.

The burners're quieter than I've ever seen 'em, too spooked for partying, so I nod off, thinking the situation's under control, until Carlos pokes me through the fence a little later, talking about a noise. I hear it, sounds like a burner, maybe two, but I can't tell where it's coming from, and neither can Carlos. The guests're all here, nobody snuck out, but still it's nerve-racking, even after Carlos checks the perimeter. I toss and turn a while longer, until first light, when I run back to the East End, only to find another body, no blood, mouth glued shut, laid out on my own bed. Okay, now this is getting bad.

That same noise makes me look up, and there're bees right above the arbor, and I'm wondering why they'd be here, when the flowers're all the way over there, and that's when it hits me: *it's them*. The bees. Makes perfect sense. They're tired of burners invading every night, taking their nectar. And with how popular the resort is, packed all the time, I can't really blame the bees for being pissed. Part of me says, but triple murder? The other part says, why not? So easy. Two or three stings, a mouthful of honey, and bam! Bye-bye burners.

It's like the bees read my mind, 'cause they take off, but I follow 'em, and they lead me right to their hive, a big one, in the base of a tree. I'm wondering how long it's been there, 'cause I swear last time I looked it wasn't. Carlos says I oughta tell Big M, and I say, 're you crazy? We breathe a word of this, we're done. We hafta solve it another way. Carlos says sorry, too late, he's pointing, and sure enough, burners're vamoosing up and down the line. Not all of 'em, but more than enough to catch the boss's attention. I'm still asking myself, how did this latest vic get off property and back on without me knowing? Then I remember the buzzing from the middle of the night, and something else hits me: if the dead burner never left, it means the attack took place *inside the arbor,* and, oh hell, if that's what they're gonna do, I don't see how we can stop it, even if we had six of me and a dozen coys.

Carlos insists the only thing to do is go see Big M, let him know what's up. Maybe he gives us the ax, maybe not, but if we do nothing, it's for sure, so at this point, we've got zero to lose. Then I find out Carlos himself won't get anywhere near Big M, and won't say why. My guess is whatever happened in Montana, he hasn't gotten over. Fine. I'll do it alone, but that coy is really gonna owe me if this all works out.

Big M sometimes visits the arbor early mornings, but hasn't in a few days, which *was* a good thing, but now I need him, and I can't wait, so I cross the property and go right up to where he's sitting, on the other side of the glass. He's looking at me, so I turn and give a *c'mere* gesture, but he doesn't move. I could tap on the glass, but that'd probably get me killed, so I do the only other thing I can. I dance.

It was something Suzy came up with, for when she was in the mood. She'd put the crown on, spread her tail feathers, and sashay her way to bed, driving me out of my mind, especially the tune that went with it. I'm wondering now if she does the same for *him*, then I remember to quit thinking so much, 'cause there's a job to do. I set up the backbeat with my wings against my sides, mark one and three with head pumps, and add the footwork, singing to myself: *One step back, two steps fore, follow these tracks, gonna see a little more.*

Suzy used to crack up when I'd join in behind, 'cause compared to her (she was such a natural), I looked like a wounded chicken. Good for a laugh every time, until it wasn't, and I shoulda known what that meant, but right now, it's my only shot at getting Big M to move, so here I am, boogying for all I'm worth. Carlos is watching through the vines, and I'm sure he's thinking, what the hell? I'm pretty far from the door, about to give up, and wouldn't you know, out comes Big M. I keep it going, one step back, two steps forward, nice easy tempo, and Big M's following, but not too close, which I appreciate, 'cause it's always a good idea to keep some distance from your boss, even if they've got a decent reputation.

He follows me into the orchard, right up to the tree with the hive, and I'm dancing circles around it, and I hear this awful sound, and there's hundreds, if not thousands, of bees streaming out. Okay, I think, this is too hot, time to cut and run. I'd rather be shitcanned than dead, and who knows what those sick bastards'd do with my leftovers. I can read Carlos's face from here, and it's not good, but the bees aren't following me, probably 'cause they know I could outrun 'em anyway, so I turn around to see what Carlos sees: Big M getting swarmed. He's running and makes it inside, and I don't know if he's gonna live or die, but it's definitely time to look for another job.

I hafta wait for the bees to settle down before I can pack up my stuff. There's not much, and all I really care about is Suzy's crown, in case she comes back, so I can put it on her head, where it belongs. (I had a crown too, a devil's claw, but I stomped it to pieces when she left.) The last of the burners're clearing out, most of 'em already gone, and then I see it—a big orange mechanical monster coming down the road, loud, toward the arbor. Jesus, I'm saying, Big M's gonna tear it all down! That was fast, I guess it means he's alive, and I better scram.

Then the thing turns west, Carlos sees it too, and trots over to watch with me, as it starts digging up pomegranates. Then there's all this smoke, and we can't see anything for a little while, and when it clears, no more bees! They all took off, and the hive's gone too, 'cause the tree it was in just got yanked from the dirt. Almost makes me feel bad for 'em. Almost.

Carlos says we're not gonna lose our jobs after all. He's right again, and I need to start listening to him more, 'cause he's sharper than I thought, and pretty cool. When I tell him what he can do to repay me for risking my life, he doesn't flinch. Imagine that, a coyote giving a roadrunner a ride on his head so I can try and win my Suzy back. What a pisser, it could actually work, and once my foot's in the door, I can show her what I got going here, and she'll be impressed for sure.

Meanwhile, the pomegranates're gone, so no more bees, and the waitlist for a reservation is even longer than before. Big M seems happy, even put up a few sugar feeders at the West End, something I thought I'd never see, but here's what it means: I get to keep spending my nights at the East End, looking the other way when the guests sneak out to get high. Works for me, now I got a soft spot for these burners, and I'm kinda hoping that Anna's comes back, the fun one, in case Suzy says no.

Okay, not really, but could you blame me? ♦

RAREBIT

In Memory of Richard G. Adams

Thaddeus's mother had survived the miracle of his birth just long enough to say his name. That she was too far gone to notice his irregularity was circumstantial evidence of a merciful God.

Thaddeus didn't know he was a hybrid—half hare, half rabbit, the only one in existence—until he finally strayed from the shallow impression in the buffelgrass. The female cottontail rabbit he met was larger than him, but not by much.

"Who are you?" she said.

Thaddeus said his name in a language he thought she'd understand.

She did, but stayed wary, staring at his mouth.

He said, "My mother looked like you, but she's gone."

"I'm so sorry. My name's Mallow." She came closer. "How do...how long have you been here?"

"Ten-ə days."

"What?!" She jumped a foot straight up.

"*Hrair*, I mean. I've been here *hrair*[1] days."

Mallow was calm again. "That was *lagilf*[2] tongue, right? But you don't look..." She tilted her head. "I guess..."

"What are you looking at?"

"Your top lip," she said, "doesn't have a split."

Thaddeus put a furry paw up to feel, comparing the single smooth form to what he saw on Mallow.

---

1 As Richard Adams pointed out in *Watership Down,* rabbits can count only to four. Any number above four is *hrair*—Lapine (rabbit) language for "a lot" or "a thousand."

2 hare

"How do you eat?" she said.

What a silly question, he thought.

"And smell," she said. "Can you...?" She put a paw up to her nose. "Anything?"

He knew what he saw with his eyes, and what he heard with his ears, and what he'd tasted with his mouth, nibbling on twigs next to his hiding place. But smell... "I don't think so."

Mallow pulled back, eyes wide, and Thaddeus learned what it was to feel different.[3]

After a short silence, she spoke again. "Who's your father?"

"I don't know."

"Your mother didn't tell you?"

"She didn't get the chance."

"What will you do?"

From her expression, he learned what it was to feel pitied.

"I don't know," he said.

Mallow turned toward the setting sun. "Follow me. If you can't use your nose, you'll have to depend on your ears. *Elil*[4] are everywhere."

A shiver ran through him, and Thaddeus learned what it was to feel fear.

At late afternoon *silflay*,[5] a few rabbits gathered near the odd-looking newcomer for gossip and speculation.

"What kind of *lagytle*[6] is he?" said one.

"Not *lagytle, lagilf*," said another.

Also heard: "He's neither, obviously." "He'll never make it with a lip like that." "His mother must be so ashamed."

---

3   Both rabbits and hares (should) have an excellent sense of smell.
4   predators
5   outdoor feeding
6   rabbit

Mallow said, "Ignore them. They don't matter."

Thaddeus was too confused to be bothered. Where *did* he belong?

She added, "All that matters is what the *owsla*[7] says."

Thaddeus nodded, though he didn't know what a council was.

"Duster and Hy and Marigold are wise and fair."

He nodded again. For the moment, being around others, even if they weren't exactly like him, was better than being alone.

He hadn't yet eaten his fill when three rabbits approached and introduced themselves.

"Come with us," said Marigold.

They went to a stand of woody bushes. Thaddeus didn't know what they were, but he knew he could eat them, and took a bite. The rabbits (not including Mallow because she'd been ordered to stay behind) looked at one another.

"Another sign," said Hy. Marigold and Duster were nodding.

Thaddeus watched them as he chewed on a branch. It was delicious.

Duster said, "Was your mother Glory?"

"I don't know. She was the color of you." He pointed at Hy. "And the size of you." He pointed at Marigold.

The rabbits looked at one another again. This time Marigold spoke. "Your mother—Glory—was banished moons ago, for..." Her cheek twitched. "Recklessness."

Thaddeus didn't understand.

"A troubled soul, she was," said Hy. "Prone to risk-taking, inviting hardship for everyone."

"*Toncinga*,"[8] said Marigold.

After an awkward pause, Duster said, "That's why we think..."

7   council

8   poison

Hy gave him a light kick.

Duster said, "We should tell him."

Hy said, "It will only add mystery to his misery."

"He deserves to know," said Duster.

Marigold said, "I thought we weren't going to tell him."

"Which part?" said Duster.

"Just the one thing," said Marigold.

Hy said, "Then what are we telling him?"

They looked at Thaddeus, who was staring back, paw over his mouth.

"Please tell me."

Hy shook her head. "I'll do it." She pointed at a bush. "See this here?"

He was still chewing.

"It's called a creosote, and we..." She pointed at herself and the other two. "...don't eat it, because we can't. But you can."

"Because your father," said Duster, "was *lagilf*."

"We think," said Hy.

"An abomination, if true," said Marigold, showing her incisors.

Without further explanation, they told him if he was ever seen in the area again, the interaction would be very different. At least they told him his father's name—or what they thought it was, because, as Marigold said through clenched teeth, they didn't follow the comings and goings of *embleer hlessil*.[9]

"Your father is famous!" Mallow had followed them into the woods, staying hidden and out of earshot until Thaddeus was alone again.

Thaddeus said, "What does that mean?"

"It means everyone knows his name."

---

9   stinking vagabonds

She went on to tell him what she knew (what she'd heard) about Lazarus, the notorious *lagomy hrair mesta*[10] and performer who held the current record for consecutive *Hare Fathers*.[11]

"They did *hrair*.[12] His teammate, can't remember his name, died soon after. An accident, they say."

Thaddeus was thinking of the similarities between his father's name and his own.

Mallow said, "You really are a half...half-and-half. That's why you look..."

She hoped he would say something.

He didn't know what to say.

She said, "This all sounds like nonsense, doesn't it?"

Thaddeus smiled and his solid upper lip dangled down over his chin, making him look like he had a *cadú*[13] on his face. Mallow laughed before turning somber. "I need to go. If Marigold catches us talking, she'll flay me."

Thaddeus still didn't know what to say.

"Find Lazarus. And may *Frith* guide you." She hopped off.

Thaddeus's fused philtrum—the reason for his inability to smell—was one of several genetic anomalies (not at all surprising, considering he had forty-six chromosomes, twenty-four from his hare father and twen-

---

10 womanizer

11 *Hare Father* is a four-paw clapping game invented and popularized by desert hares in the early twentieth century.

12 Lazarus and Jericho easily eclipsed the previous record of fifteen *Hare Fathers* when they achieved a remarkable seventeen.

13 tail

ty-two from his rabbit mother).[14] Most physical traits were expressed in an intermediate phenotype (appearance), reflecting the incomplete dominance of alleles. His time to reach maturity was four months, partway between the averages of three months for rabbits and seven months for hares. His full-grown weight, too, was intermediate—six pounds, versus two pounds for rabbits and ten pounds for hares. His sense of smell remained almost nonexistent, but was counterbalanced by enhanced efficiency in eyesight and hearing, without which he'd have had zero chance of lasting even a day.

Four months later, in mid-fall, Thaddeus found his father at sunup, nibbling prickly pear paddles in the frosted shadow of a boulder.

"Lazərus?"[15]

Lazarus knew he was looking at his son. "I been hearin about yə. Thaddɛus[16]—that *is* a name-ə. Yə mama did yə proud. A special kitt-ə, she was-ə."

"The rabbits made me leave-ə."

"They thinkin the sun-ə revolve around them-ə. Which it doesn, as yə can see-ə. Stuck up-ə buncha hole dwellers-ə. Glory was-ə differen, tho. That's why they didn-ə like her." He paused. "Or yə."

Thaddeus was already glad he'd come.

Lazarus told him how he and Glory met. "She was there-ə when me an Jɛəricho got to seventeen-ə. I saw her in the crowd-ə, and I sen

14 Mules, a much more common example of mismatched chromosomal number, have 63 chromosomes, the intermediate of a donkey (62) and a horse (64). 31 are inherited from the donkey parent and 32 from the horse parent.

15 The ə symbol is called a *schwa* and is most commonly pronounced as 'uh'. So, was-ə is pronounced 'WAS-uh', with the *schwa* syllable being equally stressed (given the same emphasis).

16 In *lagilf* (hare) dialect, the ɛ symbol is pronounced as a long A (ā) vowel sound.

her a kiss-ə, and be damned if she didn come find me-ə right after! Most rabbits wouldn do that-ə—they too good for us-ə scrawny rovers, or whatever is they call us-ə."

"Stinkin vagabonds-ə," said Thaddeus.

"Right-ə!" Lazarus laughed. "They have a way with words-ə, that I give 'em."

Thaddeus laughed too. He was surprised and pleased at how easily he and his interspecific father were getting along, until Lazarus started fidgeting and looking around like he was in the wrong place.

"Hey-ə...I gotta scamper," he said. "See yə round-ə, yea?"

Thaddeus said, "Tomorrow, yə mean? Same place-ə?"

Lazarus stood up straight. He was a good one-third taller than his son. "No, don do that-ə. Just sayin I might-ə see yə round. Whenever-ə."

Thaddeus knew it was useless to ask for more. He stayed quiet.

Lazarus said, "Go on. Get-ə movin. Yə shouldn be out in the open-ə. Yə already got so much-ə stacked against yə." He ran a paw beneath his nose in a deliberate gesture, then stood on his tippy claws, ears rigid.

"Somethin-ə comin." He crouched down. "Go-ə."

Thaddeus said, "We-ə better off right-ə here. Whatever it is-ə...is-ə movin away."

Lazarus said, "What-ə yə sayin?"

Thaddeus stretched up on his hind legs, as high as he could.

"Yə goina get us-ə killed-ə!" said Lazarus.

"No, it's aright-ə, I see it. A stag, goin toward-ə the foothills. At the base now-ə."

Lazarus stood and looked. "Yə can see that-ə far?"

Thaddeus nodded.

Lazarus sat. "And yə tellin me-ə yə heard-ə all that?" He pointed at the ground. "From down-ə there?"

"Yea," said Thaddeus.

Lazarus looked over both shoulders. "Who need a nose-ə when yə got eyes and ears-ə like that-ə?" His eyes turned to slits. "Hey-ə, I got an idea. Yə ever try-ə *Hare Father?* Yə know what I mean-ə?"

Thaddeus said, "The reason-ə everybody know your name-ə."

"Yea. Yə ever try it? Yə ought-ə. Yə might be good-ə."

"No, I..."

"Yə come from me-ə, so it wouldn be that-ə surprisin."

Not waiting for a response, Lazarus held his arms out. "Lemme show yə how it go-ə, and yə lemme know if anyone-ə comin."

Lazarus recited the rhyme a few times, until he was sure Thaddeus had it memorized:

> *Hare Father is thumpin*
> *We'd rather keep jumpin-ə*
> *Wait that's Hare Mother*
> *So let's do another-ə*

Then Lazarus went through the positions, in slow motion:

Hare	Clap[1]
Fa-	Front of paws[2]
ther	Back of paws[3]
Is	Right paw on shoulder[4]
Thum-	Left paw on shoulder
pin	Right cross high five[5]
We'd	Clap
Ra-	Back of paws
ther	Front of paws
Keep	Left paw on shoulder
Jum-	Right paw on shoulder
pin-	Left cross high five
ə	Clap
Wait	Right paw on shoulder
That's	Left paw on shoulder
Hare	Right cross high five
Mo-	Left paw on shoulder
ther	Right paw on shoulder
So	Left cross high five
Let's	Right paw on shoulder
Do	Left paw on shoulder
A-	Front of paws
no-	Back of paws
ther-	Front of paws
ə	Clap

"At the end of each time-ə thro, we go-ə right paw, left paw, right paw, left paw, to the count-ə, and it goes up by one-ə every time-ə. Get it?" He was tapping Thaddeus's shoulders back and forth.

Thaddeus said, "Like one-ε-ə...two-ε-ə...three?"

"Yea, so it get-ə harder as it go-ə. Cuz it's fast-ə, right, and the whole time-ə yə gotta be up on yər toes-ə, bouncin. It's-ə beautiful."

Thaddeus said he was ready to try, and Lazarus counted off. Having to reach up to his father's shoulders was the only part that was at all challenging for Thaddeus. They went four rounds before Lazarus stopped.

"Yeah, that's it-ə. Yə good to speed up already-ə." He counted off again, and Thaddeus matched him clap for clap with ease.

"Aright-ə!" said Lazarus. "Full on!"

When they were done, Lazarus sat back and waved at Thaddeus to do the same. "Yə..."

Thaddeus eased onto his rump, barely winded. His father's voice was tinged with glee. "We could-ə...get to twenty! I do think so-ə, cuz somethin-ə special with yə. And God-ə put us together, what yər mama use to say-ə, *Frith-ə*, lookin after me, like-ə always." He looked over both shoulders, like before. "The coyotes was-ə startin to forget-ə. Now that yə here-ə, we can remind 'em."[17]

Lazarus didn't wait for an answer. "I'll get the word out-ə, yeah? Meet here-ə tomorrow, we goina practice-ə."

Thaddeus was ready sooner than Lazarus had hoped, and in less than a month, they were standing in a small meadow at the base of

---

17 An unwritten rule of the desert: the reigning kings of *Hare Father*— Lazarus, in this case—were left alone by predators in recognition of their specialness. Everyone loved watching the hares perform and wanted to see the best of the best.

the foothills. The low, parallel ridges on either side made for excellent spectating.

Lazarus said, "Looky, they already linin up-ə. Yeah, right-ə. This'll fix-ə everythin."

During their practice sessions, Lazarus had rebuffed Thaddeus's attempts at conversation, wanting to stick to the moves and the rhymes, until Thaddeus gave up (and before he could get to the questions really tugging at him: What had happened to Jericho, the ex-teammate? And, if Jericho had earned the same immunity from predation as Lazarus, how did he die?).

Now wasn't the time. Thaddeus looked up to see coyotes, deer, foxes, raccoons, peccaries, eagles, hawks, ducks, turkeys, buzzards, squirrels, mice, snakes, and every other desert dweller imaginable. Even the bobcats, and not just the local ones.[18] A universal temporary truce, predators and prey of every stripe setting aside their position in the food chain for a few minutes, to experience the artistry and grace of the hare, one of God's most gifted creations. Thaddeus was awed and humbled by the scene. Were there rabbits too? There had to be. He scanned the ridge on the other side. Yes—he spotted Mallow, next to Marigold. He wanted to wave but didn't, in case it would get her in trouble.

Lazarus was shaking out his limbs. "Aright-ə, time to get loose-ə."

Thaddeus said, "What-ə happen after?"

Lazarus was stretching. "Assume we get to eighteen-ə, and we will-ə, yə won have a need for me anymore-ə. Yə goina be famous all on your own-ə, so we can go-ə separate ways."

"I don wanna be famous-ə."

---

18 Though hares (and rabbits) are their favorite prey, bobcats admire *Hare Father* as an art form and respect the tradition of immunity for its champions.

"Yə funny. Yə be-ə safe, yea, an everybody goina know yə. Yɛə! With that tail lookin-ə thing on your face-ə. *Nosewig*—there's a tag-ə, yea. Sound like rabbit-ə, but for yə it's *jus* right-ə."

The assembled menagerie fell quiet. Lazarus and Thaddeus faced each other, paws up. Lazarus counted off. "And-ə, one-ɛ-ə and-ə, two-ɛ-ə and-ə, three..."

Lazarus had fallen behind, a tiny fraction of a second, but they still might have set a new record, and even made it to twenty, had Thaddeus wanted. Nearing the end of their seventeenth *Hare Father,* after two full minutes of sustained athletic and mental choreography, Thaddeus stopped.

Just like that, it was over. A collective groan came down from all sides. Lazarus was staring, out of breath, mouth open.

Thaddeus ran into the bushes, with Lazarus right behind. Thaddeus stopped and turned. Lazarus was shaking his head in wide swaths, as if doing so could undo what had just happened.

"What a waste-ə," he said. "Damn if the rabbit half-ə didn come out an ruin-ə everythin. Everythin-ə!" He lowered his head to Thaddeus's level. "See yə round-ə."

Lazarus sprinted off and disappeared over the horizon.

Thaddeus wasn't afraid on his return to the rabbits' territory. Since he'd been warned (and threatened), things had changed considerably. The object of nosy whispers before, this time he attracted a crowd of eager fans, who showered him with questions about everything from his eating habits to his grooming routine. They were also calling him *Ternessi-Rah.*[19] The tallest by far, he looked over everyone's head at Marigold, who stood stone-faced with the other council members on the throng's edge.

---

19 Sentinel King

At least she wasn't scowling. He could deal with her, and the other two, later. First, he had to find Mallow. He was bursting to tell her his *other* new rabbit name. ♦

STILL STANDING

Jeremiah stood almost sixty feet tall, with six spiny arms reaching upward in balanced accord. His voice erupted. "Weather check!"

Those nearby shouted at full volume. "WEATHER CHECK!"

The words flooded like light in expanding circles, until every adult saguaro in the canyon had joined the call. (The woodpeckers were safe in their nests. It would've been earsplitting had they been out.)

Echoes were still bouncing off the granite cliffs when the shouting began again, this time starting from the perimeter. Each saguaro in turn yelled a set of climatic measurements—air and soil temperature, humidity, wind speed, solar radiation—toward the center.

Next to Jeremiah stood a short saguaro with patchy spines. Handy Andy had been stunted by a crest[1] in his youth, leaving him armless and topped with a deformity that resembled a mitt. He was concentrating on the numbers, which continued to come in until the sun had moved ten degrees past zenith.

He whispered something to Jeremiah, who bellowed. "Decrease... Ten Percent!"

This too was repeated by all.

Fifty-year-old Rowdy was halfhearted in his shout. He'd been parroting Handy Andy's orders ever since he could remember, but why? How did a misshapen old bully get to decide how much water everyone could use? Who'd put Handy Andy in charge?

Whenever Rowdy brought it up to his neighbors, they'd pretend not to hear or change the subject. No one was willing to say Handy Andy's name, much less question his purported wisdom.

---

1 Crested saguaros are also called fan-top cactuses.

Maybe somebody should, thought Rowdy.

His closest neighbor, a seventy-year-old named Chad, was an arm's length away. Rowdy said casually, "Another decrease? That doesn't sound right."

Chad said, "You know I don't like that kind of talk."

"You're right here. If not you, then who? I could yell, I guess, would that be better?"

Chad lowered his voice. "Stop it. What if somebody hears? And they tell *him*?"

Rowdy got louder. "By *him*, do you mean Handy Andy? What if they tell Handy Andy?"

Chad dropped to an angry whisper. "Are you insane? I want no part of this."

"Whatever, you spineless vegetable," said Rowdy, loud enough to be overheard. "I don't get why everybody's so afraid of him anyway. And why they think he's so smart. *I* say he's not. *I* say Handy Andy is a *phony.*"

"Now I have to report you."

Rowdy laughed. "Report me to Handy Andy, you mean? Or his big dumb sidekick?"

Chad screamed, "Report!"

The post-weather check chatter was interrupted by everyone yelling "REPORT!"

Rowdy said, "Listen up! I don't care what Handy Andy says! I'm using *more* water! Not less!" He added, "Handy Andy is a fraud! Let's try something else!"

An involuntary murmur spread like a blanket of grass.

(Elmer, farther to the north, was old enough to know what happened to the last saguaro who'd challenged Handy Andy's authority.)

Rowdy persisted. "Come on...it doesn't even look like a hand! More like knuckles!"

All were silent.

"Knuckle Head can't even do his own shouting! How can..."

Jeremiah interrupted. "To the Perpetrator!"

Rowdy said, "Come get me! I'm right here!"

(This is it, thought Elmer.)

"And what is Knuckle Head gonna do to..."

Jeremiah boomed. "Get in the Hole! And! Stay in the Hole!"

They all shouted, "GET IN THE HOLE! AND! STAY IN THE HOLE!"

Rowdy had no idea what this meant. He started to say something, but was cut off.

"STAY IN THE HOLE!"

What? It sounded like nonsense. He started again and was met with "STAY IN THE HOLE!"

Every time he tried to talk he was shouted down the same way. He got tired and decided to wait for the next day. Whatever this was would be over by then.

The cool of the morning was invigorating, as was the extra water. When the sun was thirty degrees before zenith, Rowdy whispered to Chad. "Hey, so I..."

"Stay in the Hole!"

"STAY IN THE HOLE!"

Rowdy tried again. "So I..."

"STAY IN THE HOLE!"

"Thi..."

"STAY IN THE HOLE!"

"Pl..."

"STAY IN THE HOLE!"

He took a moment to gather himself, then yelled at the top of his spines. "Gi...!"

"STAY IN THE HOLE!"

"Co...!"

"STAY IN THE HOLE!"

It was much more taxing than he'd have thought. He waited for the weather check.

At the right time, Jeremiah thundered. "Weather check!"

When Rowdy tried to join in, they all switched to "STAY IN THE HOLE!"

Rowdy knew delaying the weather check further wouldn't earn him any friends, so he let it go.

It took a few days to realize nobody would speak to him. When they spoke with one another he could hear everything, but they never mentioned him, not even a reference, as if he'd never existed.

There was also no talk of the Hole, whatever it was.

As the months passed, he made fewer attempts. It was demoralizing, being so easily overwhelmed. But how long could this last? A year? No, not possible. Still, he was beginning to wonder if he'd made a mistake.

His neighbors, who he assumed must be afraid of the Hole, kept their conversation clean, discussing things like how fortunate they all were to have such excellent guidance on their water use. By the end of the third year, when they'd still never mentioned him, Rowdy came to terms with the nature of the Hole and was sure he'd underestimated the power and ruthlessness of Handy Andy.

Five years in, Rowdy stopped trying. It was no use. He hoped good behavior, in the form of total acquiescence, might be his way out of the Hole.

In year ten, Rowdy started to grow his first arm. He couldn't ask for guidance, but he listened to older saguaros advising others about the process. He felt better than he had in a long time. Maybe he should try speaking again—he hadn't in half a decade—and besides, what did he have to lose?

He worked on what to say until it was just right in his mind. He tried a tiny hum as a warmup. Chad heard.

"Stay in the Hole!"

"STAY IN THE HOLE!"

"But I..."

"STAY IN THE HOLE!"

"Eve..."

"STAY IN THE HOLE!"

Rowdy almost died during his twentieth year in the Hole. He'd overused his water and wasn't prepared for the dry spell. He started paying closer attention to the weather check. He developed a form of respect for Handy Andy, to go along with the fear and the hatred.

His thirtieth year in the Hole, Rowdy had an especially good set of flowers. He wondered if Handy Andy had ever grown flowers. Probably not, because of the deformity. He wondered too if never having arms or flowers or fruit was what had made Handy Andy so cruel.

After forty years, some of the young adults coming up nearby had grown looser with their talk. Rowdy learned that Handy Andy was now a hundred and fifty (much younger than he'd thought), meaning Handy Andy could live a lot longer and keep him in the Hole a lot longer. Rowdy wondered if Handy Andy had ever been in the Hole. He resolved to throw Handy Andy in the Hole, someday, somehow, for good, and no matter what.

Fifty years in, Rowdy was just over a hundred, with four arms but too many woodpeckers. (They liked to burrow into him because he never shouted, and they hated the shouting.) He guessed the extra nests would take decades off his life.

In year fifty-five, Rowdy lost the memory of his own voice. Had there ever been one? It didn't matter—he was never getting out of the Hole as long as Handy Andy was in charge. Would there be a successor? Jeremiah, the assistant? If Rowdy lived long enough, would Jeremiah let him out?

At the end of year sixty, Rowdy decided to stop taking up water altogether. The neighbors could have his. Then, at least, it wouldn't go to waste.

On the first day of Rowdy's sixty-first year in the Hole, at first light, Jeremiah's voice shook the canyon. "To the Perpetrator! Get out of the Hole!"

They all shouted, "GET OUT OF THE HOLE!"

Rowdy was confused. Perpetrator?

"GET OUT OF THE HOLE!"

Then he remembered, all those years ago...the perpetrator was him! But what did they mean, *get out*? How?

"GET OUT OF THE HOLE!"

Chad whispered, "Say something, Mister Rowdy."

Rowdy tried to form a word. "Wh-wha-..." He stopped, waiting to be told to stay in the Hole. Instead, they shouted over and over: "GET OUT OF THE HOLE!"

Rowdy summoned all his spines. "Th-th-thank...you."

When the sun reached zenith, Jeremiah was quiet. So were the others. Everyone waited for the weather check, but it didn't come.

Stuck in the Hole for so many years, Rowdy had learned to listen to the silence. What he heard now was loud and clear. They might as well have been shouting, every one of them.

He said, "Chad."

"Yes, Mister Rowdy."

"Announce the weather check."

"Of course. Weather check!"

"WEATHER CHECK!"

Even Jeremiah joined in.

Rowdy listened to the data, all of it, and gave the order to Chad, who screamed. "Decrease...Ten Percent!"

"DECREASE...TEN PERCENT!"

Later, Chad said, "Mister Rowdy, will you make Handy Andy get in the Hole?"

Rowdy answered in a full voice. "I've no need to put Handy Andy in the Hole."

Jeremiah heard. "What? Why not?"

When Rowdy didn't answer, Jeremiah went into hysterics. "But you have to put him in the hole! Of course you do! Think of what Handy A... *he* did to you!"

Rowdy didn't respond.

Jeremiah's needles were shaking. "If not him, then me! Please!"

Rowdy didn't respond.

"Please, please, please! You have to put me in the Hole! I can't stay here! Not with *him*! Not for another moment!"

Rowdy didn't respond.

"All these years I've suffered! Oh, good Mister Rowdy, you are wise and kind and merciful! Have mercy on me!"

Jeremiah begged, pleaded, toadied, and even called Rowdy derogatory names until the sun was setting, ninety degrees past zenith. Rowdy made no effort to stop him.

Jeremiah lost his voice trying to get put in the Hole.

Rowdy decided to consider the request, once he'd had plenty of time to think it over. ♦

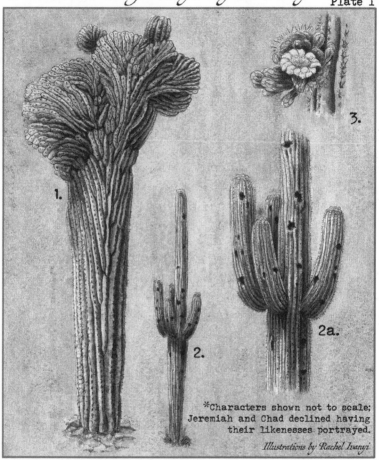

*Characters shown not to scale; Jeremiah and Chad declined having their likenesses portrayed.

Illustrations by Rachel Ivanyi

1. Handy Andy in his prime. 2. Rowdy getting out of the hole. 2a. Enlargement of midsection; indications of excessive wood-pecker activity. 3. Saguaro flower and buds. Some believe Handy Andy's inability to produce these begat his fabled cruelty.

SARINA'S DESCENT, PART I
CONCUSSION

Kyle flew right in without waiting to be asked, or even announcing his presence. Not because he was rude, which he was, but because the saguaros had struck up the Blaring[1] at five-thirty in the afternoon. (It sounded like wind whistling through the spines, but amplified to be deafening.)

Sarina was sitting on eggs in the far back. Was that Kyle? Why would Kyle be here? Nat wasn't going to like it.

Nat waited to speak until he was sure the Blaring had ended. "There's a reason woodpeckers don't come back." He said it with no emotion.

Sarina said, "So our son must have a reason to be here." She looked at Kyle. "Do you?"

"Yes." Kyle shook his head and grimaced. "The Blaring gives me headaches. Terrible headaches. And I don't have a nest."

She jumped up. "What? Where have you been sleeping?"

"In a cholla cactus. It's secure."

"But without protection from the Blaring," she said.

Nat said, "The answer is still no."

Sarina ignored him and kept talking to Kyle. "And you can't make your own place."

Kyle said, "Pecking gives me headaches."

"No, no, no," said Nat.

Sarina said, "We should discuss it."

---

1   what the woodpeckers call it when saguaros shout in succession or unison

Nat said, "This is why woodpeckers don't come back."

"Stop," said Sarina. "It would just be for a few days."

Nat said, "Kyle, give us some privacy, please."

They watched him fly off. Sarina said, "We never should've made him leave when we did. He wasn't ready."

"He *was* ready. They're all ready. They have to be."

"Except one. Out of all of them, and we're up to fourteen, Kyle was the only one who wasn't ready. He wasn't. I *knew* he wasn't, and I still made him go."

"We can't let him stay," said Nat. "It would ruin him."

"He's got no place to go. Where is he supposed to go?"

"He'll figure it out."

"He has a headache all the time. All the time, can't you tell when you look at him? It must be so hard. Do you ever think about that?"

Nat's wings sagged. "Well...alright. I'll help him." He sighed. "It shouldn't take more than three days if he does his part."

"Thank you. That's the right decision."

Nat looked out across the desert. Until recently, the Blaring had been confined to once per day, at noon, for a short period. As predictable as the sun, his whole life. Then, a few days ago, it started happening at odd times, seemingly at random, causing the woodpeckers to have to brace for it at *all* times.

Nat squawked, a short call that Kyle would recognize. In less than a minute, Kyle was back, holding his head.

"What now?" said Nat.

"Oh, it's nothing. Sorry."

Sarina said, "If your head hurts, you can tell me...us. Are you sure you're...?"

"My head is fine. I was thinking. That's all."

Nat said, "Go ahead and stay, but tomorrow, you and I are going to start making you a nest."

"Sounds amazing, Dad. Can't wait." Kyle closed his eyes. He was between his parents, who'd switched places. (Now Nat was sitting on the eggs.)

Nat and Kyle went out at dawn. Kyle already had a mild headache, but didn't say so. It would've just irritated his dad. He was going to give the wood pecking a real shot. Even though he knew how it was going to turn out. There was a reason he'd come back. His head didn't work right. It never had.

They took turns on a nearby saguaro. Nat and Kyle, back and forth, pecking through succulent flesh to wood. They were shaded by one of the cactus's arms all morning, and the only Blaring was the midday usual, which they went home for. Still, Kyle had to admit the work was causing him tremendous pain. Pain from which he could not rescue himself. He kept trying.

By midafternoon, Kyle had become ineffective. Nat suggested they be done.

When they returned, Sarina offered them fresh, plump June bug grubs from the grass at the bottom of the canyon. Kyle took his and left to stretch his wings.

Nat said, "He did fine. Up until the end. He got tired I guess." His tone changed. "I don't see how he's going to attract a mate if he can't make it through one day of shared work."

"That's not fair to him," said Sarina.

"If he can't make it on his own, we can't help!" It was unlike him to yell.

"Why don't you go somewhere and cool down? You've got a place, right?"

Nat left without responding.

When Kyle returned, Sarina told him if he kept pecking wood, he'd get a concussion.

"Dad says I have to do my part. It's two more days."

"You're going to get a concussion."

"No, I'm not. I'll be okay. It hurts, so much, but I can do it."

"You can't do anything if you get a concussion."

"Mom, I know that."

The next morning, Nat and Kyle were back at work. Nat went first.

When it was Kyle's turn, he pecked and pecked. The headache ran from the front of his face through the base of his skull. Endless pecking. Pummeling. Pounding. He couldn't go any longer, could he? He stopped and closed his eyes, imagining himself in a cloud, suspended, as if floating. What kind of cloud? How was he not falling? Why was he there?

He opened his eyes. Where was he now?

Nat said, "Kyle!" right in Kyle's ear. (Woodpeckers love doing this.)

Kyle said, "Hello? Hello? Where am I?" He was turning his head back and forth, looking confused.

Nat said, "You're with me, and we're making you a nest. You did fine yesterday. I don't know what's happening now."

"What's my name?"

"Your name? You're Kyle. I'm Nat, and you're Kyle, my son. You came back. Just for a few days."

"I'm Nat."

"No, *I'm* Nat. You're Kyle."

"I'm Kyle."

"Seriously now, are you okay?"

"Wait, I'm Kyle, and you're...Nat."

"Your dad."

"You're my dad. Right! Except I'm sure I've never seen you before."

Nat looked close into Kyle's eyes. "Don't blink." Nat squinted. "I don't see anything. But..." He backed up. "Something isn't right."

As the questioning continued, Kyle's answers turned more bizarre.

"Let the cloud carry me," he kept saying, interspersed with, "In a world full of strangers I roam."

Nat didn't know what to do. They needed to get back before the Blaring. "Kyle, follow me, okay? Can you fly?"

"I can fly?"

"Can you fly?"

"Can I fly?"

There was nothing more for Nat to say. He flew off.

Kyle went right after, but duck-hooked into the dirt, where he rolled, unhurt.

"I can do it," he said. "Let me try again."

This time he was able to follow Nat home, but missed the entrance, slamming into the saguaro and dropping to the ground.

Sarina hurried down. "Are you alright? Did you break anything?"

Kyle said he'd be fine, if he could just lie down and rest. Maybe then he could remember who he was and what he was supposed to be doing.

They all took their places in the hollowed-out den. It was almost noon. Sarina quietly said to Nat, "Did you finish the nest?"

Nat also kept his voice low. "No, we didn't get anything done today. And there are still three full days of work left if I'm doing all of it."

"You can't expect him to help you."

"No, of course not. He needs to rest."

"You think he's going to be okay?"

"Yes, yes. He will."

"He shouldn't be on his own, if he isn't well enough."

"I understand your worry."

"You know what I'm going to say next."

"Yes. That if I finish the nest and he's not ready to move in, we'll lose it to squatters."

"Better not finish it then."

"You're right. I won't." Nat looked like he was trying hard not to feel resentment. He flew off into the brightness.

Kyle said to his mother, "Well, that went fantastic."

She said, "Did you really need to crash into the side of the house?"

"It worked, didn't it? He thinks I have a concussion."

"You could have gotten injured."

"No. And you should've heard me, talking about a world full of strangers."

Sarina laughed. "I'm sure."

The saguaros were doing their thing and Nat had gone to his secret hangout, to simmer in solitude. It would be a good place for Kyle to stay, even long term, but Nat didn't want to share. And Kyle didn't deserve it. Headaches and kinship didn't entitle the boy to Nat's special things.

The more Nat thought about it, the surer he was that Kyle shouldn't have come back, under any circumstances. Head hurts, doesn't matter, can't build a nest, doesn't matter, never had a mate, doesn't matter. Kyle wasn't, and shouldn't be, Nat and Sarina's problem.

Except now, dammit, he was. ♦

SARINA'S DESCENT, PART II
CONFESSION

Abigail the mourning dove angled down toward her nest, which she and Charlie had built before their current brood arrived. Everything about the spring season had been ideal, from the rain to the gathering of materials to the acts of procreation to the egg laying to the hatching, and they were less than a new moon away from sending more offspring out into the world. This was Abigail's favorite period—the precious days spent with the little ones. Feeding them, teaching them, loving them, hoping for their future.

And sometimes, mourning them.

She could see something was wrong before she landed. Why was Lulu folded like that? Where were the others? Had they fallen?

She rolled Lulu over to see her whole face and neck coated in blood. She gasped. Lulu was dead, from a wound to the top of her head, it looked like.

She heard squeaking. Her insides froze. A child, from somewhere below.

She flew down and found her other two babies wedged in a cholla cactus, bloodied and still. She couldn't reach Elijah—the spines were impenetrable—but she could tell he was the one whimpering. And she knew Gabriel was dead by the way he was lying, even though he faced the other way. Both boys had the same wounds as Lulu.

What—who—would do this? Not a hawk, not an owl, nor any other predator. They had nothing to gain from such barbarity.

The closest she could get to Elijah was a wingspan and a half. He kept making that terrible sound as he stared back with an occasional blink. Had something happened to his eyes? Was he in shock?

She repeated his name, quietly at first, then louder, then in screams. "Elijah!" "Elijah!"

His gaze didn't change, but the whimpers got louder and more desperate, as if part of him had become aware of his mother's presence. The blood flowing from his scalp had slowed to a trickle and was hardening into branches on his neck, chest, and wings.

Charlie would be home soon, but there was nothing to be done. Abigail and her husband would have to live above their dead and dying sons until a scavenger removed the carcasses. It might take a few days.

She went back up to the nest. Lulu's eyes were open also, with the same expression. Not just dead, but...vacant.

These weren't the first children Abigail had lost, and if she stayed alive herself, wouldn't be the last. But *this*, she felt, was beyond what she should ever have to accept. Beyond what anyone should ever have to accept.

She flew high above the trees and saguaros. "I need to know what happened to my darlings!" She yelled it three times. (It was rare for doves to publicize personal tragedy.)

Later that day, a neighbor dove came to offer condolences and share what she'd seen. Charlie was home by then, too, and struggling to make sense of it.

The neighbor said, "It was a woodpecker. Male. Not sure how old, but not a kid. Big red cap. He landed on the edge of the nest and started pecking."

"Pecking," said Abigail.

"Pecking, on their little heads." The neighbor winced and took a breath. "It was the worst thing I've ever seen. Pecking and pecking, and blood spattering, and the chicks didn't even know what was happening. Two fell out, I think. I couldn't keep watching."

Abigail was calm. "Yes, two did fall. It didn't matter for them, once they were lobotomized. For us it certainly did." Charlie nodded, slow and solemn.

The neighbor said, "Wait...that's what he was doing? Going for their brains?"

"It looks that way," said Abigail.

"Oh. Oh! I hope you know, there was nothing I could do. I mean, it was a woodpecker..."

Abigail shook her head. "Don't worry, really." She looked at Charlie and back. "But is there any chance you know where he came from?"

"No, but maybe someone does. I can help you find out. If you want."

"That would be appreciated. Thank you."

Two days later, Abigail went to see Sarina the woodpecker, arriving just after dawn and waiting a few swoops away until the two adult males had flown off. (*Two* adult males? That was strange.) Abigail darted over and perched at the entrance to a hole that was halfway up the saguaro's thickest arm. "Hello?" she said.

"Can I help you?" said Sarina.

"Yes, I..." Abigail stepped into the cool darkness. "I know it's unusual for a dove to be here, but these are unusual circumstances. My name is Abigail. May I proceed?"

"Of course. Sit over here. In case the Blaring starts up."

"The blaring?"

"Er...never mind, sorry. Where you are is fine. I'm Sarina, and go ahead."

"I know who you are. Day before yesterday, when I came home with breakfast, I found two of my children dead and the third brain-dead. Attacked by a woodpecker, according to witnesses. From what I've been able to figure out, the woodpecker who did it lives here." She looked around the den. It did seem small for three adults and the three chicks in the back.

Sarina said, "I can't imagine!"

Abigail nodded, waiting.

Sarina said, "So you think this...monster...came from here. The other two residents are my mate and my son."

Abigail twitched. "Son? I thought woodpeckers didn't come back."

Sarina let her irritation show. "It's only for a short time, and none of your concern. You were saying, someone murdered two of your children?"

"My *three* children, yes. The third died last night, finally, while being pulled from a cactus by a rat. We couldn't get to him, you know. His name was Elijah."

"That is...I'm very sorry."

"I know it's not unheard of for woodpeckers to prey on young doves, especially during shortages. But to suck out their brain and nothing else is wasteful. Senseless. And to leave them alive, even worse. It's cruel. All because of some stupid myth."

"What myth is that?"

Abigail tilted her head. "You know what I'm talking about."

Sarina tilted her head in a mirror image. "No, I don't."

"Squab[1] brain. As an aphrodisiac."

Sarina thought for a moment. "I swear, I have never, ever heard that."

"Fine. It doesn't matter."

"I'd assume whoever it was, did it for the fluids."

---

1 fledgling bird

Abigail jumped up. "Fluids? Look around!" She lowered her voice. "Sorry to get excited, but we're not so distressed that we need to be sucking newborns' brains out of their heads."

"It *has* been a wet spring."

Abigail sat back down. "I don't know what else to say. I guess I was hoping you, as a mother, would understand."

"I do, and I'm glad you came, and I agree with you *one hundred percent*. I'll look into this, but I can guarantee you, neither of the males I live with are capable of what you've described."

Abigail wanted to say, "With all due respect, they *are* woodpeckers," but kept it to herself.

Sarina said, "I guarantee, not capable."

Abigail said, "You seem decent, and I appreciate your time. In conclusion, someone in your household might not be so decent, and I thought you should know." Before Sarina could argue, Abigail went on. "And I was hoping you'd put a stop to it, if you can. Out of mercy, or pity. Or whatever it takes. My children aren't the only victims, either. It's gone too far."

Sarina appeared to soften. "I'll do what I can. Thank you so much for telling me." She was quiet as the dove shuffled out.

Abigail went back to the empty nest that was stained with her children's blood. Charlie was there, waiting to comfort her. He offered to build a new place by himself, somewhere else, but Abigail said it wasn't necessary. She had reason to hope her entreaty would be answered. She'd made a connection with another mother, hadn't she?

As soon as Nat returned home, Sarina asked about the baby doves. Did he know of anyone who might have been doing anything like that? (Nat hated when she asked in a manner that implied an accusation.) He angrily denied involvement, then suggested it could have been Kyle, who'd been coming and going at all hours.

When Kyle was confronted by his parents, he claimed absolute innocence and pointed a toenail at Nat. "It was *him*! I saw him do it!"

Nat said, "What?"

Sarina said, "What?"

Kyle nodded, breathless. "It was Dad. I saw. I wish I hadn't, because of the nightmares. I can't shake them."

Nat said, "What you're saying is simply not true." He turned to Sarina. "He's making this up. I would never..."

"I believe you," said Sarina. She looked at Kyle. "Maybe you saw someone you *thought* was your dad. It happens with woodpeckers."

Kyle said, "Yeah, that must be it." Sarcasm gave way to earnestness. "It also feels like someone's setting me up so they can kick me out. And I haven't done anything wrong. I mean, aside from little stuff."

He stared back over his shoulder as he flew away. (Something woodpeckers do when they've been offended and want everyone to know it.)

Sarina and Nat both shrugged. She said, "Somebody that looked like you."

"Must be."

In the late afternoon, Nat brought snacks for the little ones. Sarina was going out for a fly-around after spending most of the day in the boot.[2] She said, "Need anything?"

"No. But Sar, I hope you believe it wasn't me, with those babies. I wonder if it wasn't really Kyle. It's odd that he would tell such a blatant lie."

"I was wondering about that too. I don't think Kyle could've done it, though. He can barely peck wood."

"I don't know, those skulls are really soft at that age. Look at our own little..." Nat shook his head, like he realized he was rambling. "Okay,

---

2   a woodpecker nest in a saguaro

you know what? Confession time. I'm going to level with you. Right here and now. Are you ready? It *was* Kyle. Our son did it. All of it. I watched him."

"But he says the exact opposite."

"He's lying. I saw with my own eyes. It was so horrible, sweetheart, I didn't know how to tell you. That's how horrible it was."

Sarina flew away in disgust, knowing with absolute certainty that neither Nat nor Kyle had killed those nestlings.

She'd left a rose petal for herself in the main vee of a nearby palo verde. She retrieved it in her beak and wiped it against a newly torn branch that oozed with sap. She put the petal down, sticky side up, and placed the top of her head against it. Crowned in red, she looked from any distance like an adult male Gila woodpecker. She was on her way to see someone. ♦

SARINA'S DESCENT, PART III
CONDITION

It was still well before sundown when Sarina showed up at Yonas's boot, which was spotless and elegantly accented as usual. (Hoarding was a common problem among older widowed woodpeckers, but not Yonas—his place would've made a nine-month-old bachelor proud.) Sarina took extra care in removing her petal bonnet, pinning it to the floor with a toe and lifting her head, by degrees. (The time before, she'd done it too fast and lost a few plumes off the very top. She told Nat she'd gotten carried away mining a beetle from a log.)

"Stop," said Yonas.

Sarina looked up. "You want me to leave it on? Sir?"

"Yes."

She raised her head. "Why, sir? May I ask?"

Yonas walked a circle, inspecting her up and down. "No, you may not." He stuck out a leg, putting light pressure on her underside. She shuddered.

"Can you feel it?" he said.

Her breathing quickened. "Yes."

"Yes, what?" His tone had an edge.

"Yes, sir."

He applied more pressure. "You've done as I ordered."

"Yes, sir." She was quivering.

"It's been more than a day since you drank the tonic?"

"Yes...sir..."

"Good girl. And you arranged to be absent for an extended period?"

"Yes, sir."

"You please me, Sarina." She was grinding against his thigh. He pulled away. "We're in no rush, then."

She wobbled.

He said, "Show me your cloaca. I want to see if it's true what they say."

She turned, tilted her rear end up, and looked back at him. He was slack-jawed.

He leaned closer. The ring of flesh was distended and paler than normal, almost white. "My Woods," he said. "What does it feel like?" He touched it.

"Like nothing I've... ever..."

"And the fragrance..." He paused, inhaling. "I'm going to take good care of you, Sarina."

"Please, sir. I'm ready.

"Do something for me first."

"Anything, sir."

"I want you to leave a smear."

Without hesitation, Sarina went to the back of the room and, starting at the floor, rubbed her hind end up the wall as high as she could, standing on the tips of her nails.

"You *are* ready," Yonas said. "As am I."

She held the swollen donut out like a gift. He moved her tail feathers aside, climbed on her back, and pressed his own cloaca against hers. She gave a raspy chirp. He said the sound pleased him and ordered her to keep making it. The chirps turned into a persistent, guttural call. He rubbed harder and faster.

"Thank me," he said.

"Thank...sir...thank...you."

"For what? Be specific." He pulled away.

"Oh no, don't stop...!"

"You first."

"Uh...oh...thank you, for...showing me...who I...*am*?"

He resumed vigorous grinding. "You've been so good, it's time for you to move in with me."

Her body stiffened. "Yes," she said. "Yes!"

"Yes, what?" He yanked her tail feathers.

"Yes, sir! Yes, sir!"

"And you will do as I command, always."

"Yes, sir! I will!"

He peeled the petal off with his beak. "You won't need this anymore."

Sarina couldn't have responded if she'd wanted to. All four inches of her tongue had unwound from her skull and were dangling from her beak like a monster grub.

Yonas said, "Are you alright?"

She nodded.

"That's the most amazing thing I've ever seen."

Sarina couldn't hear. She was lost in the *Endless Forest*, a state of woodpecker rapture reached by only a fortunate few. (Most, in fact, doubted its existence, including Yonas, until now.)

He stayed on top of her, prolonging the cloacal kiss,[1] until exhaustion made him quit. When he slid off, Sarina's organs began slowly shrinking to their normal state and position. She was waking, as if from a long sleep. She was aware she'd been in an altered state. She was aware she'd discovered—and shown—a side of herself she hadn't known existed.

Wild with desire, she'd...

She'd...

---

1   avian (bird) intercourse

The mourning dove, the mother...no...

(It *was* abhorrent, even by woodpecker standards.)

Yonas took responsibility. "It was I who led you down the path."

"But I still...did it." The shame was coming in waves.

Yonas forgave her with orders to forgive herself also. "You need to learn how, Sarina. It's too important."

"Yes, sir, thank you, sir."

"You took the tonic *for me*, is that clear?"

"Yes, sir."

"And I will never ask it of you again," he said. "I promise."

"Thank you, sir, thank you. I couldn't do it again."

"Tell me that I am kind and generous."

"You are kind and generous."

He tugged on a downy breast feather.

"Sir," she said.

"Very well. Is our time up?"

"A bit longer, sir."

He scratched her back. "Let me tell you how it's going to be when it's just us."

Seventeen days later, Sarina announced to Nat and Kyle that she was leaving. They were shocked. (It's not easy to shock a woodpecker, much less two.)

Nat said, "We just kicked our latest brood out of here *this morning*."

"That's why I waited," she said.

Kyle said, "You're leaving me too? What am I supposed to do?"

"You've got your dad," she said. "You two have each other."

Kyle said, "I didn't fake a brain injury so you could abandon me again!" He flew off, glaring back for so long that only a last-second swerve kept him from crashing into a century plant.

Sarina said, "Fake brain injury? What's he talking about? Do *you* know?"

"Don't go," said Nat.

"I have to. You know that."

"I don't know that. I don't. And it isn't right. We're supposed to mate for life."

"I shouldn't be chained to you forever just because that's what woodpeckers do."

"What about Kyle? What am I supposed to do with him?" He sounded desperate.

"Like I said, you have each other."

There was silence for a few long minutes. Sarina was thinking about an exit when Nat wailed. "You can keep the lover! More than one! Mate with them all you want! I don't care! But please don't leave me!"

She edged toward the opening.

Nat stood taller. "Your choices have consequences, Sarina. You know that, right?"

"Yes I do."

"If you go now, you are *never coming back*. Is that understood?"

"Yes."

"If you show up here, I can't guarantee what I will or won't do."

"Be nice to Kyle" was the last thing she said.

Flying to Yonas's with no disguise should have been liberating and joyful, but Sarina felt vulnerable. What if things didn't work out? And the guilt! Had she done it for Yonas or herself?

She stepped inside. Yonas looked like he'd been waiting. "Is it done?" he said.

"Yes, sir. I belong to you now."

"You always belonged to me."

"Always, sir."

"Excellent. I've got more tonic for you. It's not too late in the season yet."

"What? Sir?"

"You heard me. What I saw last time, I need to see again. One day from now."

"I can't do that, I'm sorry...sir."

"It's not up to you, Sarina."

"You said never again. You promised."

"If you expect to stay here, you'll do as I say, and call me sir."

"Can we drop the *sir* thing...for a moment...? Because this isn't right. You can't turn that awful...the part you *know* I regret...into a condition."

"Actually, Sarina, I can, but you know what? It doesn't matter. There are plenty of other woodpeckers around. Younger, more beautiful, more open-minded. Yours isn't the only funk on the wall."

"That was mean. And unnecessary."

"We had an arrangement."

"And all the talk about our future?"

"It was part of the arrangement, and if you didn't know that, you should have."

"I have no other options. Because of you."

Yonas turned away and didn't see her leave.

Sarina sat low in a blooming acacia, ruminating. She couldn't go back to Nat, though she knew he'd let her in. When he found out the truth—and he would, someday—it'd be impossible for him to understand, or forgive. Her thoughts came back to Yonas, and her pain hardened into fury.

She was thinking about where to stay when the Blaring began. There being no immediate shelter, she flew straight up, high enough so the sound didn't rattle her eardrums. She'd just reached relief when she had to drop out of the way of a huge flock of doves moving through the clouds. Unusual, them being so far up, and it wasn't because of the Blaring. (They couldn't hear it. Saguaros and woodpeckers were the only ones who could.)

The doves disappeared. Sarina flew in circles, her fury ripening into a thirst for revenge, until the roar of the cacti abated. ♦

SARINA'S DESCENT, PART IV
CONFLAGRATION

Sarina wanted to fly by her old (since that morning) nest, for a peek. To make sure Kyle was there. Maybe she'd disguise herself with another rose petal. Tucking her wings, she went like a missile down to the canyon.

From a thousand feet, she could tell something was wrong. White was scattered all over. Not so much on the ground, but on the larger cactuses and trees. Lots of woodpeckers were out and darting around.

As she crossed five hundred feet, the saguaros started screaming again. No! Why? Was it related to the white blotches? Now everyone was rushing back to their boots.

Sarina's head hurt. She knew how Kyle must feel, if he was telling the truth. (Being a woodpecker, he probably wasn't.) Closer to the ground, the noise was unbearable. She had to go *somewhere*, just until it was over. Nat and Kyle would understand.

Her senses had been too preoccupied to notice the smell, but in the relative quiet of the boot, she knew right away what it was.[1]

"Dove shit," she said.

Kyle was wide-eyed. "Mom? What's happening?"

Nat said, "Yes, Sarina, why are you here?"

Sarina said, "I don't think that's what he meant."

Kyle started to speak but Nat cut him off. "I don't care what he meant. I want to know why you're here."

"There was nowhere else."

---

[1] Woodpecker noses are just as keen as their eyes and ears.

Nat raised his voice. "I understand you needed protection, but why *here*? Why not with your new *mate*?"

Sarina put her head down. "He's not my mate."

"Sure he isn't. You're a piece of work, you know that?"

Kyle said, "Can somebody please tell me what's going on? The saguaros won't stop and there's poop all over. I even got it on me." He leaned sideways to show them. "I can't see it, but I smell it. It's so gross!"

He kept whining as Sarina scraped off what she could with a small stick.

Nat said, "I'll tell you what. I don't know about the cacti, but the doves made a big mistake."

Sarina didn't get it—why would doves think vandalizing woodpecker homes was a good idea? Didn't they know what *always* happens when you hit a woodpecker? (They hit back twice as hard.)

Nat said, "We'll put a response team together asap. Those winged rats are going to wish they'd never been born."

Kyle said, "What'll we do to them?"

Nat said, "Hit back. Twice as hard." He looked at Sarina. "And you... can leave any time."

"Wait," she said. "I'll go, but listen—I know why they did this."

"Nothing to do with mutilated babies, right?"

"Stop. I know how to fix it, too."

Nat shook his head. "The only way to *fix* this is to bring a conflagration." He turned to Kyle. "We're woodpeckers, son. It's what we do."

Sarina said, "I'm going to find that dove, her name is Abigail. Kyle, come with me."

Kyle said, "But it's too loud. I can't go out there, you know that!"

She tried to steady him with her eyes. "Staying might be worse."

Nat said, "We *are* going to stay, right here, until it's safe to leave. Then we'll join the others in...my Woods, the stench!" He made a gagging sound. "...in avenging this heinous, filthy act."

Sarina rested a forearm on Kyle. "You don't want any part of that. Come with me. We can fly straight up and over and wait to come down."

Kyle said, "I'm staying with Dad."

"Really?" Her wing slid off his back.

"Dad's never lied to me. And *he's* never left me."

Sarina stared at the floor.

Nat said, "I know about the bogus concussion, also." He looked at Kyle. "Thanks again, son, for telling me."

Sarina said, "I thought it was real!"

Nat said, "Right. It doesn't matter, because Kyle and I now have an understanding. And you're not welcome here, so if you have anywhere else to go, please do."

Kyle frowned. "Yeah, Mom."

Sarina stooped to avoid the droppings on her way out.

The Blaring didn't let up for a long while. It had to be a response to the guano, but in celebration or despair? The first three doves she asked for directions scuttled off, before a young hen who knew Abigail (but didn't know any better) told Sarina where to go.

She touched down hard next to Abigail and Charlie's nest. Charlie readied to stand but Abigail nudged him. "Don't. She's not staying."

Sarina said, "Hear me out. Please."

"We can't stop you," said Abigail.

"Thank you. I just wanted...I know who's responsible for the murders, so you don't have to blame all of us. And..."

Abigail cut in. "We'd love to know, of course, but at this point, it's beyond our control."

Sarina continued, "...and to warn you, we're coming. You need to pack up and leave now, while you still can."

The doves looked at each other.

"Listen to me," said Sarina. "Whatever you *thought* you were going to accomplish, all you did was infuriate a bunch of woodpeckers."

Charlie said, "But those are just the markings, the..." A squint from Abigail made him go silent.

Sarina said, "Markings?"

"It's nothing, and too late anyhow," said Abigail.

Sarina said, "Okay, never mind...I'm telling you...things are about to get *really ugly*."

Abigail said, "I'm going to share this with you because we're both mothers, and I'd want to know." She paused. Charlie rearranged himself.

Sarina said, "Tell me what?"

"Our petition was finally accepted. By the city pigeons. We're cousins, you know."

Charlie said, "They don't usually accept petitions. Very rare."

Abigail said, "Only under the most extreme circumstances. I suppose these qualify."

"*You* convinced them, dear," said Charlie.

"Because it hasn't stopped, and it won't stop, until we make it stop," said Abigail.

Sarina said, "City pigeons...what the Woods are you talking about?"

Abigail said, "The markings are to identify the targets."

Charlie said, "You think we're dumb enough to..."

"Quiet," said Abigail. "They should be getting there about now. A whole squadron, I understand. That's what I meant by too late."

Targets, markings... Sarina caught her breath. *They'll be buried alive.*

Rachel Ivanyi.

The Blaring was back, louder than ever, and as Sarina came over the last ridge, she could see why. It looked like a blizzard had swept through the canyon. The trees and cactuses were slathered with layers that would take days to dig through. Any woodpeckers still in their dens were done for. What about Nat and Kyle? Her head was pounding. The stink, too, was debilitating, like lightning in her nares. Other woodpeckers were out, but aimless. Like her, they were trying not to picture their loved ones suffocating in ammonia tombs.

Getting to Nat's, her hope dimmed. The cactus arm she'd been in her entire adult life (since meeting Nat five years before) had fallen off under the weight of so much excrement and was lying on the ground under a mountain of white. Maybe...maybe Nat and Kyle weren't inside...maybe they'd already left to go...where? Where? She couldn't think straight. Yonas...huh? Why think of him? She stood on a boulder next to the reeking pile, trying to *survive* the noise. She needed to fly up and away, but not without...

Suddenly, but for a few trailing echoes, the desert was quiet.

"Mom!"

She turned. Kyle was sitting on a branch, next to Nat. They looked perfectly fine. Sarina remembered. "Your special spot!"

"The one you made fun of," said Nat.

"Never again." She flew up to them.

Nat's voice was cold. "Nothing's changed. Between you and me."

"Thank you for protecting him. It's why I chose you in the first place—your huge heart."

Nat said, "He and I can stay in the hideout for now, until all this gets rained off."

(Which could take a long time.)

"What about the doves?" said Kyle. "And those awful pigeons?"

Nat said, "Pigeons are too big, too strong. Especially the city types." (Woodpeckers are many things, but not suicidal.) "We'll figure out what to do with the doves later, after we assess our losses."

Sarina shouted in his ear. "Nathan!" It startled him. "Please," she said.

"*What*, Sarina?"

"I can still fix it."

"That's what you said before. *Now* look."

"Come, and I'll show you. After that, you'll never see me again. I promise." She looked at Kyle. "Please?"

"I'll go if you do, Dad," said Kyle.

"So...?" said Sarina.

"Alright, fine."

The Blaring buckled the ankles of all three. Nat pointed up. "Let's go!"

It was two hours of circling before the next window.

They showed up at Abigail's late in the afternoon. Charlie let out a panicky whisper. "We're through!"

Abigail replied in a plain voice. "No, we're not." She gave a slight nod to Sarina. "I see your relations made it."

"Many weren't as lucky," said Nat. "Too many. Children, infants, entire families. You birds are going to *pay*." His voice cracked.

Abigail said, "I know how you feel. I should have a nest full of little ones right now, but..." She was still looking at Sarina. "...they died for someone's sick satisfaction instead."

Sarina said, "It wasn't me! But I know who it was!" She took a breath. "I'll show you, and we can end this before there's any more killing."

Abigail said, "We're listening."

"Can you follow me? It's not far. If the Blaring starts, we'll have to go high and wait it out."

Abigail said, "You're talking about that...sound. Are you saying it's *not* happening right now?"

"Not at the moment, but..." Sarina didn't want to reveal how much the Blaring was working in the doves' favor. (If they didn't already know.) She took off, and the rest followed: Abigail, then Charlie, then Kyle, then Nat.

Yonas's giant boot was near the top of one of the tallest saguaros at the high end of the canyon. Sarina poked her head in and saw him resting comfortably. "How'd you not get hit?" she said.

"Lucky, I guess. And I mind my own business. Something you might try, Sarina." He stood up. "Nevertheless, I'd love to know why you're here. Change of heart?"

She stepped inside. "I wanted to make sure you knew what you caused."

"I can see from here. But it wasn't only me, was it?" He sharpened his tone. "Why *are* you here, Sarina?"

She moved aside, and Abigail entered. "Oh my, this is...what a gorgeous home!"

Sarina said, "He's very proud of it. Aren't you, Yonas?"

Yonas was focused on what was happening at the entrance. The dove who'd come in uninvited was followed by a male dove and two male woodpeckers, all of whom looked very upset.

"What's going on?" he said. (With six adult birds, the place was now jam-packed, blocking most of the light.)

Abigail spoke. "I'm told *you* are the one responsible for the slaughter of our brood."

"I have no idea what you're talking about. I'm just a senior pecker, living out my last days in peace and quiet."

Abigail tilted her head.

"He's a liar," said Sarina. "I know, because...one time...I was there."

Nat bumped his head on the ceiling. "You *what?*"

"He tricked me."

Yonas said, "Can we talk about this outside?"

Abigail said, "You're sure it's him."

Sarina said, "I swear on my all-time favorite son." She looked at Kyle.

Yonas was trembling. "She's lying! It was all her! She's sick!" He pushed toward the exit, but Nat and Kyle stood firm.

Charlie said, "Who do we believe?"

"None of them," said Abigail. "They're woodpeckers."

"Excellent advice," said Nat. He looked at Sarina, who looked at Abigail.

"You know what to do," said Abigail.

Yonas said, "Wait..."

"We'll be outside," said Abigail. She nudged Charlie. "Come along, dear."

Charlie said, "Um...is it alright if...I stay and help?"

"Not...no, no—!" Nat and Kyle closed Yonas's beak and held it shut with their elbows.

Sarina said, "He's welcome. In fact, we'd love to have him."

Abigail looked at her husband, her black eyes reflecting what little light there was in the den. "Enjoy."

"I love you, honey," said Charlie.

"And I you too."

"Mmnh...nnph...!"

Abigail stepped into the brightness, leaving enough room in the boot for three angry woodpeckers and one very enthusiastic dove to tear Yonas apart, limb by limb, then bone by bone.

(Blood on a woodpecker signifies a debt paid. With nobody wanting to take on the pigeons—and by extension, the doves—three bloody woodpeckers were adequate cover for all of them to lay down their arms.)

"Well, this is it," said Nat. He'd brought Kyle *and* Sarina to his hideout, low in the trunk of a mesquite tree and surrounded by prickly pear.

Sarina said, "What's going to happen with you and me?"

Kyle said, "You guys want some privacy?" He sounded hopeful.

"Sure," said Nat. "Thanks."

Kyle flew off without looking back.

Nat stared at Sarina for a long time before he spoke. "I haven't asked you to leave yet."

"I've noticed."

"I *am* curious about one thing."

"What's that?"

"The brains. Baby brains..."

She nodded. "The tonic, you mean."

"Okay, yeah, the tonic. Did it actually...work?"

"Why do you ask?"

"Just curious. Like I said."

She went to him. "I mean...I could, you know...after all this blows over." She moved closer. "We could go far away and...I could...you know."

"It *would* give our boy a chance to be on his own a little. Get accustomed. Exactly what he needs."

Sarina's eyes were half-lidded. "And I was thinking...since we're alone...I could tell you more about...you know."

She looked ravishing, caked beak to talon with her lover's blood.

"You read my mind," he said. ♦

WOLF!

They stood in a tight group on the meeting ledge. They needed to move to a bigger one, but were still evaluating options. Should they plan on their number continuing to increase and choose somewhere with room to grow? Or find just enough for now, in the spirit of humility? The Gods, it seemed, felt favorably toward them, a disposition they wanted to maintain.

They didn't mention Lorna's alleged sighting of the wolf.

What? They didn't even bring it up?

They didn't bring it up and they didn't believe her. Lorna had already been pegged as oversensitive and alarmist, never mind that she'd just seen her sister get taken by a lion, her sister's skin giving way like a succulent to keratin[1] scythes.

No—there was no way Lorna had seen a wolf, they determined. None of them had *ever* seen one, nor had any of their ancestors, as far back as they could remember. The Gods wouldn't be so cruel as to send them a wolf *now.*

I saw a wolf!

Lorna knew what was happening: the others were so terrified of the truth—that there *was* a wolf—they were unable to consider it. The problem was the hot panic Lorna had felt in her veins, millennia of avoidance baked into fifty-four strands of bighorn sheep DNA. *She just knew.*

There will be more!

Whereas a lion could kill one or two ewes, a pack of wolves was an extinction-level event waiting to happen.

---

1   what claws, like fingernails, are made of

Why aren't they worried? They should be!

The others reassured Lorna of the Gods' love and understanding. The Gods would not have sent them a wolf. Not after moving them from the old country.[2] Not after giving them a new life in a place with more water and more protection from the sun and more ways to escape from lions. Not after the Gods had shown Their love by killing the lion that had killed Lorna's sister. Had Lorna forgotten? The Gods punished the lion for what it had done. The Gods are smiling on us, they said. Life has never been this good, they said.

But it was a wolf!

Lorna insisted they had to tell the rams.

To warn them at least!

The rams had heavy horns for their own protection, and they could protect the ewes, too, but the rams and ewes were separated by a considerable distance.

It's too far! The ewes are easy slaughter! And the children!

The others reminded Lorna of their Covenant, to stay away from the rams except during the times of procreation.[3] Why would she risk angering the Gods?

Because of the wolf!

Before, whenever Lorna closed her eyes, she'd seen a lion pulling the red meat of her sister from white bone. Now, she saw the wolf. The yellow eyes and the outline of silent breath. A new terror, infinitely more dangerous than the last.

She couldn't allow the inevitable by doing nothing. She left early, before the sun was up. She knew it was more than half a day's journey.

---

2   near Yuma

3   Male and female bighorns live apart most of the year and come together for mating season.

As for whatever repercussions there might be from the Gods, what could be worse than the wolf They'd already sent?

The rams were not expecting her.

Why on earth are you here? they said. You have violated our Covenant with the Gods by coming now. You have no idea what damage might result.

There was a wolf, she said. I saw a wolf!

Are you sure? they said.

She was sure. A wolf! The herd needed to come together—she pleaded—so the rams could protect the ewes. But the ewes hadn't believed her, none of them, and she'd had to trek alone. She was only doing what anyone else would've done, if they'd seen a wolf.

Some of the rams were convinced this wayward ewe had already angered the Gods. In a meeting, they proposed a sacrifice. Most of the rams were opposed, and the motion was voted down. The ewe would be sent back to her own and treated for confusion.

Because of his youthful strength and agility and his easygoing demeanor, Robb was chosen to escort her.

Lorna was no less agitated than before.

I'm telling you I saw a wolf!

And Robb kept saying no, that's not possible. The Gods wouldn't have sent us a wolf. Not now.

It could be right here! She was watching, watching.

No, he promised her. No. He asked about what she'd seen, to be kind.

It stared at me through the branches of a juniper, she said. Like a vision straight from my nightmares.

He said, how do you know it wasn't a coyote? They come up here sometimes. And it's good to be aware of them.

He might as well have asked her if she knew the difference between a rock and a tree. There was no reason to discuss it further.

She knew the way as well as he did, if not better. Near a water crossing, she went toward a patch of grass that had been chewed.

Don't, he said. Don't touch anything out here, they told us. Remember?

She remembered. Because it could be tainted by the goats who are familiars to the Gods, they'd said. She also remembered eating from the same patch on the way over. She kept that memory to herself.

She was watching always for the wolf, even though Robb said there was no wolf. He tried to persuade her, but she was insistent.

Robb is wrong! They're all wrong!

Lorna was very unpopular when she rejoined the ewes. She might have angered the Gods, and for what? The illusion of a wolf, which everyone knew she hadn't seen. Then, when Lorna was the first to become ill, they talked about blaming her if it was the onset of a plague.

Lorna got better but Robb didn't. Too sick to return to the rams, he stayed with the ewes, set apart, until he died. When ewes started dying, the rest believed they'd fallen out of favor with the Gods. This was a plague sent to express anger and disapproval. And to punish.

You made us sick, they said to Lorna. You made all of us sick, even the rams. All because you believed the Gods had sent us a wolf. And now look.

The meeting ledge was no longer crowded. The remaining ewes decided the only way to deal with Lorna was a sacrifice.

It felt very unfair to Lorna. They were blaming her for the plague, and they didn't even know about the patch of grass! All because she went to tell the rams, which is what any of them would have done, *if they'd seen the wolf.* But they still wouldn't believe her.

Lorna was afraid of the sacrifice.

I'll be alone with the wolf!

It was set for the following morning. Lorna opted for higher ground because she believed the wolf was likely to stay lower. (She had no reason to think this.)

When it got dark, she found a spot to make a bed. She felt totally alone, except she knew she wasn't, because the wolf had to be watching her.

The wolf has been watching me this whole time!

Since they first saw each other through the branches of a juniper.

I saw the wolf and the wolf saw me!

She was certain.

(It could have been a fox, or a coyote, or a ringtail, or a coatimundi, or a bear, or any number of things, but not a wolf, because there *are no* wolves in the Santa Catalina Mountains. Not now.)

Lorna was eaten by coyotes that first night. Her sacrifice didn't help; the rest of the herd, every last ewe, ram, and lamb, died from the bacterial infection Lorna had picked up by eating the wrong grass.

The Gods are thinking about what to do next. ♦

METAMORPHOSIS

Her chances of making it to adulthood were close to zero.

The day after her parents met, Polly and her approximately four hundred siblings wriggled free of their translucent casings. They shared a temporary pond—a large puddle that appeared only during a heavy rain—with tens of thousands of other spadefoot toad[1] offspring. All but a handful had entered life's lottery with a losing ticket.

The newborn tadpoles swam together in a giant school, one of nature's oldest and most reliable protection strategies. It worked for most, but not all; the least fortunate two percent were taken by a diving beetle larva in the first five minutes.

After days of nothing but algae, Polly ate her first brine shrimp by accident. Right away she wanted more. The tiny arthropods were plentiful, and she gorged herself with impunity. Her head grew wider, as did her mouth. Her two rows of teeth went from nubby to sharp. The next beetle larva that swam down to fill its belly got a rude welcome when Polly ripped it apart. It was even tastier than the shrimp.

More.

As far as she knew, she was the only one of her kind who'd developed a taste for meat. She went to the surface and found a variety of floating insects to fulfill her cravings, which were more intense by the hour. She could breathe air now and hold it in for as long as she wanted. She was beginning to feel invincible.

She didn't realize she'd bitten the tail off a fellow tadpole until she saw it flailing and sinking. She gobbled the rest, starting with the head.

---

1 Commonly referred to as toads because of their appearance, spadefoots are neither frogs nor toads.

Any who weren't her siblings became the next course on her menu. It took three days to eat them all.

Her cartilaginous cranium had doubled in width again, and she eyed her brothers and sisters. What good were they? None at all. She was growing fast, needing more and more food, and the puddle had already shrunk by half.

By the time the remaining water had evaporated, hardly any tadpoles—now froglets—were left. They'd grown legs and lungs and might have been able to walk out had Polly not eaten them as they writhed against one another in the mud.

She finally left her birthplace in the middle of the night. She was nine days old. Adult spadefoots were everywhere, male and female, and Polly's mouth had grown wide enough to swallow them whole. When the sun rose, she used the keratin shovels on her back feet[2] to burrow into the sandy soil, tail first.

For weeks she hid by day and hunted in the dark. Once she happened upon a centipede, orange and leggy. It stopped screeching when she crushed its head in her jaws. On another occasion, attracted by a new and pungent scent, she found a dead pack rat. She tore at and swallowed the fetid meat (and accompanying maggots and flies) with relish.

She grew and grew and grew.

When the first dog went missing from the park around Silverbell Lake, nobody was concerned. Dogs ran off all the time; it was another reason to keep them on a leash, aside from respect for municipal codes and one's neighbors.

Those who saw the homemade signs assumed the dog was either disgruntled or lost and would turn up eventually, as long as he didn't try to cross one of the busier roads. Then a second dog went missing, and

---

2   hence the name spadefoot

a third. Still, there was no general alarm, until a young woman vanished from the same park. She'd last been seen jogging by the lake.

Panic swept the community. Escaped convict? Registered sex offender? Was there a connection to the golden retriever and two mutts? The story dominated the local news, because whoever had done this was *still out there.*

The sheriff's office and scores of solemn volunteers searched in widening circles from the park, finding no trace of the woman (or the pets). There were tips and suspects and even an arrest, but every lead came up empty. Recovery divers scoured the bottom of the shallow man-made reservoir—seven feet at its deepest—for nothing. With no physical evidence and no witnesses, investigators started looking at the missing woman's relatives, including her parents. In these types of cases, experts said, the perpetrator was often a close acquaintance of the victim. The national networks picked up the story, and professional talkers who knew none of the facts demanded action.

After two months passed without another disappearance, human or otherwise, everyone but the family went back to their routines, and law enforcement considered putting the case in the cold file.

Nobody actually saw the creature rise up and grab the five-year-old boy, who'd been fishing with his father at dusk. All they remembered was the child being pulled by the head while attached to a bench via harness and leash. (This little boy had a history of trying to wade in.) The father grabbed his son's legs and the animal—whatever it was—twirled and retreated beneath the surface. The father was left holding a twitching, headless corpse.

The two witnesses, who'd looked over only when they'd heard a scream, said it was an alligator. The father, when he was finally able to talk, disputed their claim. "It was right in front of me," he told the sheriff. "That was no alligator."

It might have been the size of one, a big one, he said, but it had smooth skin, a flat face, and a wide mouth. He noted odd protrusions behind its jaws that looked like seaweed, or leafy kale. The sheriff brought in a naturalist and an artist, and when they created a sketch of what the father thought he'd seen, it resembled a giant salamander, complete with external gills.

A study of the bite marks showed the injury had been caused by two rows of teeth that were narrow, short, and needle-sharp at the tips. The animal had literally ripped the boy's head off, having scored his neck with hundreds of punctures.

This time they drained the lake. Still nothing. The Silverbell Monster, as it was being called, had somehow escaped. Thinking it might have burrowed down, they dug into the bottom with equipment from a nearby mine.

They were on the right track. They just didn't go deep enough.

Earlier that summer, the low-frequency vibration of the first monsoon raindrops hitting the ground above had announced: *It's time.*

Polly's mother[3] had spent the past ten months in a moist cocoon of her own dead skin, losing half her body weight, so of course she was ravenous when she crawled to the surface. First, though, she needed to evacuate her uterus.

The humid night air was dominated by the sound of male spadefoots trumpeting their case:

Pick me!   *I'm the fittest!*   *You're the fairest!*

You're the one I've been waiting for!   *Pick me!*

---

3   Polly's mother, remember, was a spadefoot.

All you need is me!   All I need is you!   We're meant to be together!

Pick me!   The others can't compare!   Pick me!

She found three potential partners floating nearby, their throats ballooning white with each call.

She chose the one with the brightest spots.

He crawled atop her from behind as they treaded water, but before the mating process could begin, one of the other males swam over and knocked him off.

She waited for whichever of the two wanted her more.

The interloper got on her back and locked his arms around her gut, just above her hind legs. He croaked his readiness.

She began releasing her eggs in cylindrical masses, which he fertilized the instant they came out of her cloaca.[4] When she was finished, all she could think of was food. Winged termites to be precise, her favorite, and after a rain like this, they'd be plentiful.

But *he* wasn't finished. He wouldn't let go.

She kicked with rising anger, trying to gash his hind legs with her spades.

His grip tightened. What was he doing?

Between the fasting and the physical toll of ovulation and oviposition[5] she had almost no energy.

More! More! More!

She didn't have any more! He needed to let her go! Now! Right now!

She wiggled and thrashed, trying to throw him off, but he was too strong. Where were the others? Why didn't they help?

---

4   This is called *amplexus* or frog sex.

5   egg laying

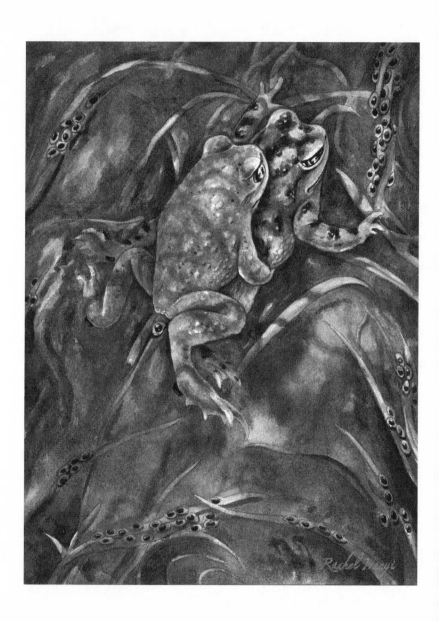

Stressed and desperate, she was able to squeeze out one last egg, which her attacker bombarded with the remainder of his ejaculate before finally letting go. He slid off her back, satisfied.

Nine days later, that final egg had metamorphosed into Polly, who didn't know that her parents were among the dozens of spadefoots she devoured her first time out of the puddle.

It wouldn't have mattered. She was hungry. ♦

THE NEOTENIC QUEEN

Getting the opportunity to put down roots for the Family was a dream come true for daughter 62,229. And how lucky she was to have a pair of wings *and* a pair of eyes! Unlike most of her subterranean siblings, who'd been granted neither.

Still, she was only *one of thousands* of termites about to take the Flight of Destiny, as Mother and Father[1] called it. There were so many questions: What would the air feel like? And the light? How would she know when she met the right partner? She stood in the packed tunnel, waiting for her turn. What was taking so long?

Growing up as a winged nymph, she'd never had to assist in path building or foraging. Her life had consisted of lounging in the royal chamber, being groomed by ordinary workers and fed by them too, either mouth-to-mouth or anus-to-mouth. (She wasn't allowed to choose menus or mealtimes—Mother and Father controlled all that—but she never went hungry.)

She didn't mind the sounds and smells of her parents copulating (it was always pitch dark underground), because Mother was so full of children, and Mother and Father were both so full of nourishing Love for the Family. The copulation had become less frequent since the recent onset of Mother's illness, which both Father and Mother insisted was temporary and nothing to fear.

The line had stopped moving. Why? Alerts rippled down from the front. Death! Death! Everywhere is death! At the same time came a clear message from Father: *Keep going and Love will protect you.*

---

1   Mother and Father are depicted on the front cover.

Daughter 62,229 expected Love from Mother too, but there was none. Mother must be too sick! It had to be the reason, and daughter 62,229 no longer wanted to leave. She wanted to stay with Mother and Father. Others could seek the twin glories of parenthood and expansion. She was most needed *right here*, with her Family.

Too late! Daughter 62,229 was swept upward, expecting any moment to see the brightness, until she remembered there was no sun yet, because the exodus had begun in the middle of the night. But the dryness of the outside atmosphere was unmistakable. Her translucent skin toughened and darkened in response.

Alarm pheromones filled the air, and there was no trace of Love. The termite soldiers with their square heads and straight pincers had formed a defensive circle around the hole, doubtless following a strategy Mother and Father had laid out, but giant-jawed beasts[2] whose slick red bodies gleamed in the starlight had broken through the line. Daughter 62,229 watched in horror as scores of her sibling *alates* (winged nymphs) were carried off in squealing, writhing bundles.

None of the *alates* had ever flown, but their bodies knew what to do. Daughter 62,229 rose with other survivors in a swarm, leaving the carnage below. The lightest breeze jostled her, making her think she was going to crash. Flying was hard! Not knowing where she was going, or how high she was, she focused on staying horizontal until she was ready to give the signal.

The signal! Because she couldn't put down roots by herself, she needed a mate: a Father to her Mother. A tiny drop of liquid oozed from a gland on her forehead. It smelled like home. Within seconds, a male was hovering in front of her, trying his best to entice. Was he the one? They touched antennae.

2   ants

No, and she'd gained enough control of her wings to be able to turn away.

Another male appeared, also hopeful. Was he the one?

No.

Many tried, a parade of dozens, but she chose none of them.

Daughter 62,229 stopped secreting. She was worried about Mother and Father, especially Mother. She knew what she had to do. Her thinking was clear! As if a dense fog had lifted. She'd always felt a special connection to her parents, and now they needed her help with the Family. Because Mother was so ill!

She slowed the beating of her wings until she began dropping. Wait, too fast! Steady, steady, she floated to the ground. Having no idea how far she'd drifted, she spun in a slow circle. Three-fourths of the way, she detected the scent of home. Hooray! It wasn't far. But she was afraid of the melee around the hole.

The monsters had been replaced! A new one,[3] wider than five holes, was using its giant mouth to scoop up both marauders and defenders alike. The *alates* were all gone, having flown away or been pillaged. Daughter 62,229 broke her wings off at their perforation and, leaving them behind, ran past the remaining termite soldiers on the perimeter and down into the nest.

The humidity and the familiar smells were comforting in spite of the chaos. Three times she had to squeeze by piles of dead soldiers who, at Father's command, had committed mass suicide, so as to block the tunnels. When she finally reached the royal chamber, she was overjoyed. Mother! Father!

Father demanded to know why daughter 62,229 had returned. (He'd never shown anger toward her before.) She'd been *chosen* to put down roots and grow the Family, and now this? How could she? Her

---

3   spadefoot toad

wings—where were they? She was supposed to keep them until *after* she'd chosen a breeding partner! (Their simultaneous shedding of wings before building a nest was how future Mothers and Fathers committed to exclusive, everlasting Love.)

Mother came to the defense, reminding Father that daughter 62,229 had been designated from birth as a possible neotenic[4] replacement for Mother. It wasn't unheard of for *alates* who'd started out as contingent reproductives to have mixed feelings when leaving.

Neotenic replacement? Contingent reproductive? Daughter 62,229 absorbed the meaning. Of course! It finally made sense, the special connection! She'd been raised to succeed Mother! She'd always known she was different from the others, but hadn't understood how or why until now. So why hadn't they told her before?

The lucidity she'd experienced outside was turning into numb contentedness. Because of Father. His Love was powerful and sustaining, but daughter 62,229 didn't want to be numb anymore. If she could think on her own, she could maximize her Love. Especially if she was going to be the next Mother.

Mother died the next day. Her massive abdomen provided an historic feast for everyone except daughter 62,229, who was too nervous to eat. It was the moment she'd been waiting for. She'd been born for this! Would there be a ceremony? When? Would Father want to meet in private first? The possibilities were enthralling.

Father made the announcement before Mother's remains were digested. He'd chosen a new reproductive partner, but it wasn't daughter 62,229. Daughter 62,229 was given the honor of chief caretaker of daughter 343,343, who was hereinafter to be thought of and referred to at all times as *Mother.*

---

4   retaining juvenile characteristics in adulthood

Daughter 62,229 was shocked and furious. How could Father do that? Daughter 343,343 hadn't undergone her first molt. An infant! Why hadn't Father chosen daughter 62,229 instead? Was she too old? But how could that be, if she wasn't even a year! Was it because her skin was no longer supple or translucent like it once was? It hadn't been her decision to go outside. (No decision had ever been hers!) She'd been forced, as part of her obligation to the Family. And what about Mother? She'd been outside. (It was how Mother and Father met!) Mother's skin had been hard and crusty, and she'd been *old*, too, older than anyone in the Family except Father. Father should want—and have—a replacement for Mother who was *more like Mother*. Not an ignorant child who would never grow wings and never leave the room she was born in.

Daughter 62,229 set about nurturing the neotenic queen, which meant feeding and grooming her around the clock. Father was content, the young queen grew, and, like every other member of the Family, daughter 62,229 did her duty.

Or so it seemed. In reality, from the beginning daughter 62,229 had been feeding the usurper (daughter 62,229 refused to think of her charge as *Mother*) from her anus instead of from her mouth. Consequently, the queen got plenty of nourishment, including the protozoa she'd need in her adult gut to help with digesting cellulose, but she wasn't getting the hormones necessary to stimulate sexual development.

Father was frustrated that daughter 343,343 couldn't mate yet, because he needed a new partner right away. The ambush of the Flight of Destiny had left the Family at its least populous since year zero. Father transferred daughter 343,343 to the ordinary workforce and chose daughter 351,152 to replace Mother. And this time he chose *someone else* to be caretaker. He'd begun to suspect cracks in daughter 62,229's devotion and sent her to the ordinary workforce as well. Her time in the palace had come to an end.

The bond daughter 62,229 thought she'd shared with Father had shriveled. Father had done that! With his mind. He'd given her the ability to Love him, then he'd yanked it away. And he'd already tried to send her off once, into the maws and jaws of predators! What more evidence did she need? She wasn't wanted. Not anymore. She'd been used, like all the others, *like Mother even*—and the rest of them had no idea, because their minds were so filled with Father's Love, which she could see now wasn't *love* at all. It was *control*.

For the first time, daughter 62,229 regretted coming back. Her eyes and her already half-dissipated knowledge of the outside world were useless. But with more time in the tunnels, far from Father, her thinking regained some of its earlier clarity. Because of the distance! Hooray! As long as she didn't get too close and took care to eat only certain meals, she could remain unpersuaded by Father and his evilness. *Now* she knew: when to eat from other workers' mouths, when to eat from their anuses, and when to forage for herself. Her sexual organs, which had withered since her return, began to blossom again, and Father didn't know, because he was many rooms away and had more important things to think about, including the newest innocent he was trying to turn into Mother.

A few weeks later, daughter 62,229 gave her first order to a soldier. The secretion she'd released many times before usually meant she was hungry, but this time, a soldier, its head so big it almost filled the tunnel, came over and stood at attention, waiting for instructions. Daughter 62,229 was curious about the status of Father and his new queen, and the soldier ran off to find out.

By the time the soldier returned, daughter 62,229 had attracted a group of them, a dozen at least, all of whom seemed ready to fulfill her wishes. And just in time, because the news was troubling: daughter 351,152 was about to begin laying eggs. At which time she would truly become Mother.

Daughter 62,229 couldn't allow it, because it *wasn't right*. Not for Father, not for Mother (less so in death!), not for any of her bewitched siblings, not for daughter 351,152, and most of all, not for daughter 62,229. Something had to be done. Fortunately, Mother's *rightful successor* was willing and available.

An attack from within was neither expected nor prepared for. Most of the soldiers were still out guarding and cleaning the perimeter, and those few that had stayed with Father were easily overwhelmed by the rebels. Daughter 62,229 was secreting from her front and rear glands in unison, letting Father and everyone else in the Family know: *she* was a mature reproductive female. The neotenic queen—daughter 351,152— tried to respond with secretions of her own, but she was too young, and too small, and too soft, and, as became obvious to all present, including Father, *too weak*.

Father needed a Mother, and he needed one right away, or the Family would face annihilation. He expressed his rage in secretions that shook the foundations and every tunnel of the massive home they'd built. Daughter 62,229 touched antennae with a soldier next to her. The neotenic queen was cut in half, squealing in the way a termite does, until the soldier sheared twice more.

Before Father could respond, daughter 62,229 went to him. She was almost his size now, the result of her raging sex hormones. She laid her first egg. Father scampered to her rear and fertilized it. She laid another. She thought about a particular food she wanted. It was brought to her. Then she wondered—how many more neotenic reproductives were there?

When she found out there were still two remaining, she ordered them sliced to ribbons also, but in another room, because of the noise. She signaled the soldiers to help themselves to the carcasses, in reward for their loyalty. Meanwhile, Father didn't seem to miss Mother or his

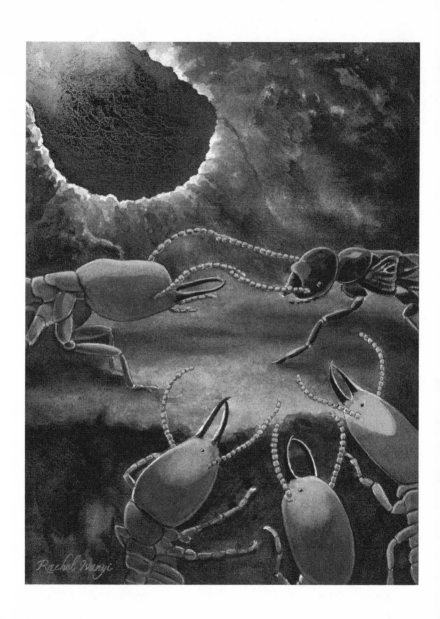

child brides. Had they ever even existed? He seemed perfectly content repopulating the Family with daughter 62,229.

Later, Father suggested several nymphs be set aside as potential replacement queens, as a precaution. He was reminded he needn't concern himself with such things any longer. Daughter 62,229—*Mother*—was in control. Her abdomen had expanded, she was laying more eggs, and her ability to *share her Love* with every member of the Family grew by the minute.

Father kept trying to reassert himself, as if unaware of any other possible course. How pathetic! And annoying. He was old, tired, and *replaceable*. Why couldn't her eggs be fertilized by a young, energetic, male reproductive with clear, smooth skin (because he'd never been tarnished by the outside air)? What a pleasant idea! She chose two fresh nymphs, showered them with her Love, and designed for them a special menu, so either one would be able to replace Father before the change in seasons.

If Father didn't like it, he could take it up with the soldiers. ♦

THE STIGMA

The birds were late.

Angi[1] had gone from superstitious to super concerned.

Flo wasn't worried at all.

Bud wondered how many berries Flo and Angi had, but wasn't good enough with numbers to guess.

Phyll[2] was excellent with numbers and could've gotten within a percentage point, but didn't try, because Angi was so worried.

They all knew what each of the others was thinking.

Because her berries had already gone from red to translucent, Angi was trying to remember if the silky-flycatchers, who ate until their stomachs were bursting, had *ever* been late.

Flo thought the delay was historically cool, because when the silky-flycatchers *did* come, they'd be super hungry.

Bud still wanted to know how many berries there were.

Phyll, the eldest and largest of the four desert mistletoes who lived in the same mesquite tree, kept coming back to: *There's a first time for everything.*

The hundreds of other mistletoes in the canyon thought collective didn't dwell on it, knowing a mass consideration of possible negative outcomes could trigger a mass panic.

Angi believed: *You don't count your berries until they're plucked.*

---

1   short for angiosperm (flowering plant)
2   short for chlorophyll

Flo thought Angi's adages were silly and dated.

Bud was starting to worry.

Phyll was calm. *This too would pass.*

Phyll was wrong.

Angi didn't understand why *all* the responsibility for growing, ripening, and delivering the berries lay with only *half* the collective.[3]

Flo agreed it was an issue.

Bud was happy to try and do more, if asked.

Unlike Phyll, who knew better. All he or Bud—or anyone else who had stamens[4] and no stigma[5]—could do to help was: *stay cool.*

(Every mistletoe was imperfect[6] and thus could not bear fruit alone.)

Angi thought Phyll and Bud and the others with no stigma should donate part of their uptake of water and nutrients, just until the silky-flycatchers came.

Flo didn't need it (yet), but wasn't opposed.

Bud was willing.

Phyll thought those who bore the stigma *must bear it for a reason.*

Phyll's logic became the standard justification for making zero sacrifice on behalf of those who bore the stigma.

Angi put off *knowing* her berries were overripe as long as she could, because of existential terror.

---

3   Only female mistletoe plants produce berries.

4   male flower parts

5   female flower part

6   In botany, *imperfect* means having only one set of reproductive organs, i.e., male or female.

Flo was alerted to the crisis of her own berries—losing sugar every second of every minute of every day—and the silky-flycatchers *still hadn't come. And if they didn't soon...*

Bud perceived an unfamiliar disquiet.

Phyll concentrated. Because of his stature as one of the most experienced mistletoes in the collective, the others would follow.

They sensed Phyll was more worried than he'd ever been—through droughts, dust storms, floods, locust infestations, and even the root-borne tree virus that only by working in disciplined unison were they able to eradicate.

Angi didn't know what to do.

For the first time, Flo was as worried as Angi.

Bud was pretty sure Phyll could get this figured out.

Phyll came to the preliminary conclusion they were all *doomed,* and it rippled through the collective.

Three days after the silky-flycatchers *should have* shown up to gorge themselves and spread sticky seed all over the canyon from both ends of their digestive tract, somebody thought they heard one imitating a quail.[7]

Angi was pretty sure it was an actual quail.

Flo couldn't tell.

Bud was too deep in dread to notice.

Phyll agreed with Angi.

---

7 The species of silky-flycatcher portrayed in this story, *Phainopepla nitens,* can imitate the calls of a dozen other birds, including Gambel's quail.

The bird that sounded like a quail *was in fact* a quail, as useful to the hemiparasites[8] as a dead host.

Angi wondered what in the world was keeping the silky-flycatchers away.

Flo did too.

Bud focused on what Phyll was thinking.

Phyll wondered what Angi and Flo had done to make the birds *not want* their plump, juicy, nutritious, delicious berries.

The concept gained instant traction with about half the collective (the male half), which blamed the other half for the disaster.

Angi knew it wasn't her fault.

Flo wasn't as sure.

Bud didn't want to think about it.

Phyll believed there was no denying the facts: *after* the harvest of light, *after* the parade of insects, *after* the polyamorous exchange of liquid and powder, *after* fertilization had begun, *something had happened.*

There was no way to prove Phyll wrong.

Angi knew holding fruit for much longer would kill her.

Flo understood what Angi was thinking but couldn't personally relate.

Bud was trying to figure out a way to make his own berries.

Under normal circumstances, Phyll would have thought Bud was a moron and mocked him.

---

8 A hemiparasite is a partial parasite. Mistletoes use chlorophyll (hence the green color of the plant) to photosynthesize sugar from sunlight while getting water and other nutrients—things they'd get from the ground if they grew there—from their host tree.

These were not normal circumstances.

Angi suggested that maintaining all these berries might be so taxing as to kill the whole tree.

Flo was starting to feel the strain herself.

Bud didn't want to die.

Phyll made a proposal: To acknowledge genuine differences of opinion and to streamline communication, Phyll would think on behalf of the males and Angi would think on behalf of the females.

Phyll's proposal was unanimously accepted.

Angi didn't know what would happen if all the berries were dropped on the ground, because nobody knew.

Phyll thought this demonstrated exactly why it should *not* be done.

Angi tried to convince Phyll she was more valuable alive than dead.

Phyll tried to convince Angi the berries had *no value* if the silky-flycatchers didn't want them.

Angi heard a darker implication—that *she* had no value.

Phyll did not deny the implication.

A day later, Angi dropped her berries, as did every other bearer.

Phyll thought it was a tragic error in *judgment*, one that would *haunt them forever.*

Angi was glad to be free of the burden.

Phyll questioned whether they should even bother with any more polyamorous exchanges, if those who bore the stigma weren't going to hold up *their end of the bargain.*

Angi agreed there was no reason to continue the current arrangement.

All communication between the factions ceased.

Angi and Flo extracted as much water and nutrients from their host tree as they could, believing Phyll and Bud would do the same.

Phyll and Bud did the same.

Every mistletoe in the canyon doubled in size in half the usual time.

Angi and Flo knew their host was dying.

Phyll and Bud knew it too.

Angi had a plan: *more flowers.*

Flo didn't have any better ideas.

Bud was already aware of Phyll's alternate plan, but didn't want to give up his flowers.

Phyll's plan: forego flowering, once, to be in a better position to compete with Angi and Flo for resources.

The following spring, all those who bore the stigma (and one who didn't—Bud) produced their most aromatic flowers ever.

Angi was prepared to die.

Flo still didn't grasp the gravity of the situation, but was one hundred percent loyal to Angi.

Bud liked his flowers but knew he was in trouble.

Phyll recommended Bud be expelled from their faction, as punishment for *creating discord.*

Bud was expelled from their faction.

Angi and Flo welcomed Bud to theirs.

Bud was glad, because Phyll's weird views and tendency to disapprove had bothered Bud for years.

Phyll's view: *Good riddance* to all of them.

The remarkable fragrance drew a new kind of being. Bigger than a silky-flycatcher, much bigger, it was stuck to the ground like a tree but meandered like a bee. And it was *noisy.*

Angi knew right away when the branch she lived on was severed, removing her access to water *immediately and forever.*

Flo felt Angi's loss and wanted to follow.

Bud was lying on the ground next to Angi and Flo before he knew what was happening.

Phyll was spared, because he didn't have a fragrance.

Every mistletoe who bore the stigma (and Bud) were gathered up and taken from the canyon.

Angi liked how they were all crammed together and moving.

So did Flo.

Bud was hyperaware of his uniqueness, but liked the togetherness too.

Phyll didn't matter anymore.

The parade of insects came.

Angi and

Flo and

Bud enjoyed a polyamorous exchange with a bunch of strangers who didn't seem to care if Angi and Flo and Bud were attached to a live host or not.

Phyll was happy to be rid of them. He had a tree to himself, and there were stamens everywhere—and *no stigma.*

Without access to water, Angi and

Flo and

Bud died soon after joining their new collective.

They are not forgotten.

Phyll lived a long life, dying with his host of natural causes, *the only way to go.*

Nobody ever figured out why the silky-flycatchers hadn't come. ♦

ALIEN SPACE BATS

When we, the Zarmorians, first got to Earth, fifty-two million years ago, the Bromundians[1] were already here. They—and just about everything else—were having sex, lots of it, and as part of our *blending in* strategy, we did the same.

"I've learned to like it." Kendra was talking about sex. "Love it even, sometimes. When it's good. Know what I mean?"

"I don't. I've never bought in."

"Maybe you haven't been in the right situation."

"Maybe." I doubted it.

On a more immediate topic, Kendra was insisting I shouldn't tell the Commandant the truth.

"Don't do it, Liz. He's only here to see the land perverts on parade. This is not a policy visit."

"I wouldn't be doing my job if I didn't tell him." And it wasn't just hearsay: I'd seen the fungus *on a transmitter* with my own eyes.

(There was a belief among transmitters that we were immune because, officially, none of us had ever gotten the disease, even though so many millions of our tailless cousins had. It wasn't my fault such a belief existed, nor was it my fault the belief turned out to be erroneous. I was just reporting.)

Kendra said, "Have you met him before? The Commandant?"

"What? No."

"Well, take my advice. Stick to the easy stuff. And try not to stare."

The penis that hung past his knee when he was right-side up. "I've heard about it."

---

1 beetles

"Commandant-sized, for sure."

"Terrific."

Kendra was right about the hard-not-to-stare part. I guess that's how one becomes such a high-ranking official in the Zarmorian military. I almost didn't notice his tail, which was impressive too, just not in relation to his mammoth penis. And speaking of tails, the Commandant told me the land perverts—*Homo sapiens*—still didn't know about the embedded communications equipment, because apparently, it's too small for them to see. What morons! (One sad thing: most of us have never actually gotten to transmit. We get sex, sex, sex, all the time, but no transmissions.)

Like me, the Commandant had a tail, which placed us in the twenty percent of bats (earthborn Zarmorians) who were transmitters. And he'd grown up in the area, which was why I thought he might listen, even during an off-the-record, friendly, apolitical stopover.

His conversation was standard for an officer. "We're up to fifty billion warriors, and the land perverts have no idea. They estimate our number at a fraction of what we really are. I predict it will be very few generations before we advance to the next phase."

He was talking about the attack phase, where we turn every species on the planet into a managed food source. (The sort of thing these late-career military types live for, and you just know there've been hopeful officers saying those exact words for hundreds, if not thousands, of generations.)

The Commandant and I were now hanging upside down from the Campbell Avenue bridge, near one end, above a crowd of gawkers on the path. I said, "You're not worried about the fungus? What if it *did* come from the Bromundians?"

He stared at me. The tip of his penis was resting on his chest, almost touching his chin. "I'm mostly here to see the land perverts in clusters," he said. "Like these." He waved a wing at the group below. "This is still one of the best spots on the entire continent, no?"

"It is, Commandant."

"And call me Leonard, please. I insist."

"Sure. Leonard."

As if he *hadn't even heard* my very legitimate questions. I wanted to scream. Kendra was right; unless it was good news, the Commandant—Leonard—didn't want it. We barely talked the rest of the show, but I kept catching him looking at me. (I assume to see if I was checking out his penis, which I wasn't.)

He did deliver a few good one-liners, like when he described an obese land pervert as a dancing scarab beetle after a transmitter flew too close. I took the tangential opportunity to share my personal belief that the white-nose syndrome—the official name of the fungus—had come from, and been manufactured by, the Bromundians, in retaliation for an insect virus *allegedly* introduced by our side three centuries ago.

Leonard acted offended. "You don't have any actual knowledge, do you? That we had anything to do with the beetle scourge?"

He shouldn't have been irritated at the topic, because it was *he* who brought up beetles, not me. Either way, I assured him, I didn't know anything. I'd just thought he might like a little color with my reporting.

"Observations only," he said.

"As you wish." He wanted me to stay within the lines of my job—reporting what I'd seen in the territories. But he didn't *really* want my observations. He wouldn't *really* want to hear about all the places I'd found infections. He wanted me to tell him everything was fine. As if my actual job had no actual meaning.

Maybe it was spite that pushed me over the edge. I'm not sure and it doesn't matter. I told him about the old transmitter in Texas, with her

whole muzzle and chin and even her elbows covered in white. (It had an odd smell, the powder. I'd noticed it on the others too.)

His expression changed. "A transmitter with the fungus? You're sure?"

"Sorry, but yes. Totally sure."

He gave himself a quick fondle while watching the last of the land perverts returning to their vehicles in the twilight. "I'm going to pretend I didn't hear that." He looked at me and smiled, his fangs reflecting red neon. "Let's party."

Kendra had told me about this too. He'd assume because he was a commandant with a rock star penis and I was just a government reporter, I'd want—or feel obligated—to have sex with him. If he assumed that, he'd be wrong, and besides, there were more important things to worry about. Didn't he need to tell his superiors about the first fungal infection in a transmitter having been *verified*? If transmitters were to get sick in large numbers, millions of years of preparation would be in jeopardy.

"This could be a disaster," I said.

He spoke more quietly. "I didn't hear that either." He wasn't smiling any more, and his penis looked like it might have shrunk a little.

"It's too late," I said. "Too many others know. How about we alert the right official so we can forget about it, and maybe come back here. To party." I could wriggle out of it later.

Had I ever actually transmitted? He wanted to know. No, was my answer.

"It's not bad at all," he said. "I mean, it's not sex or anything." He looked at his penis. "Later, later." Like he was talking to it. Kind of endearing.

"Alright," he said to me. "Come. If we're going to war with the Bromundians anyway."

We flew above three thousand meters, and I'll say it was *too chilly* up there.

I didn't realize what was happening at first. My tail was wriggling around, like it was looking for something, then it locked onto a signal, and I could feel the information going from my brain, out my tail, and straight to the home planet. Every detail of the sick transmitter and her powdery visage. Not just information, but *feelings*. How I felt about seeing her illness, then and now. The transmission satisfied me in a way I hadn't known I'd been missing.

Leonard was nodding. "Yes."

"I had...didn't..." was all I could say.

I thought of how worried Leonard must have been about his superiors. This was *bad news* they were getting. Very bad. By Zarmorian nature and custom, they would blame the Commandant. And punish him.

Might he might try and shift the blame to me? Was that why he brought me along? After all, *I* was the one who'd seen a transmitter with the fungus. *I* was the bringer of such worrisome tidings.

He transmitted after me, and when he finished, he said he'd taken all the responsibility himself. I asked him what that meant and he didn't want to discuss it, though he added I had nothing to worry about with respect to my own situation.

Later on, he told me he had one more night as Commandant before he was demoted, so he wanted to enjoy himself and prepare for the rest of his life as a simple worker. We were right side up, and he looked at me with a claw pointing to his penis. "I'll still have this, though. So, there'll be opportunities. But enough about the future. Let's talk about now. Want to party with me my last night as an officer?" He stroked the long, soft leg hair beside his scrotum.

I thought about what Kendra had said. Was this the right situation? There *was* something about him that seemed genuine. Sincere. And he *was* still the Commandant, technically. Plus, he *did have* a magnificent penis. (I'd be lying if I said it didn't interest me at all. Kendra had said it was okay to be depraved, too, like the land perverts. It made sex better, she'd said.)

I like to imagine the land perverts sitting around, and the looks on their faces when they finally figure out what they've been calling "bats" this whole time are actually space aliens, and we've been competing for mastery of their planet with "beetles," who are also space aliens.

Hold on a minute, they'll say. Bats are mammals! Like us!

Live young? Check. Lactation? Check. Body hair? Check.

Corrupt minds and variable penis size? Check and check.

Okay, wings. What about wings?

(No answer)

Oh yeah, not only can bats fly around like bullets, they can avoid things at high speed *in the dark*. Like some kind of superhero.

(It's because they're aliens!)

When a billion Doberman-sized fruit bats with an insatiable appetite for mammal flesh appear out of nowhere, the land perverts will *really* understand. (It's mind-boggling how many bats, even the biggest ones, can crowd into a square meter.) ♦

THE FALL OF JERICHO

When one of our most celebrated athletes dies young, everybody wants to know details. Not just how and why, but whose fault it was, because nothing bad happens in the desert without its being someone's fault.

I've heard at least a dozen versions of Jericho's demise, ranging from implausible to bizarre. A few examples:

He ran into a tree in the dark at full speed.

He fell into the river during a rainstorm.

He was playing with a bear trap. (My favorite.)

In all of these, Lazarus, Jericho's *Hare Father* teammate, is somehow to blame, which isn't surprising; that's what happens to survivors around here. It didn't help that after setting the record, Lazarus and Jericho went high profile, reveling in the fame and glory, and the immunity, that came with being champions.

Don't believe any of it. I'll tell you exactly what happened, because I was there. You can decide for yourself whose fault it was.

It wasn't mine, in case you're wondering. I'm not interested in jackrabbits anyway; they're lean for my taste, and small, even the athletes. I prefer peccaries any day, or bighorns, or mule deer, or the ultimate, livestock.

I was warming myself in the morning sun, minding my own business, when Lazarus sauntered up, asking if I knew who he was. I understand what immunity means—in fact, as a mountain lion, I'd say I have the last word on the subject—but this jack was *bold*. Any prey animal that's approached me before has ended up dead because, frankly, I don't care. They move a certain way, I flick a paw, and it's over. I've no need to show mercy, or fairness, or even consideration.

But I digress.

If Lazarus was afraid of me at all, he didn't show it, and it wasn't for lack of perception on my part—I'm an expert on fear, and his bravado interested me enough to keep my paws to myself. And although I hadn't attended the performance (I never go to those things; my presence is too disruptive), I did know his name, because word had already spread from the Santa Ritas to the Catalinas about Lazarus and Jericho and their historic run to seventeen.

The intrepid jack had a proposition for me: I keep him protected, and he'd show me some of his secrets. Secrets? What? I had no use for learning their little parlor game, as beautiful as it was to watch.

It's nothin like-ə that, he said. He was talking about real knowledge that could and would be useful. I gave my tail a silent swish and told him I was listening.

He was right to question the extent of his immunity. The previous champs, who'd held the record for six years, both perished under mysterious circumstances, but not until after a good long stretch of freedom. Imagine, as prey, getting to spend even a few days walking around in broad daylight without existential worry. If it doesn't last forever, who cares? I'd take the promise of a year or two over none at all. The rest of the desert wakes up every day or night thinking it's probably their last.

Lazarus said *I* was the one who could make it so he never had to worry, because *I* was in charge, and whatever *I* say, *go-ə.*

"Tell me more," I said.

Lazarus asked if I could catch a hare. It seemed like a silly question, seeing as I've caught plenty.

No-ə. I mean-ə on a dead-ə sprint.

That seemed silly too. Nobody can catch a jack on a dead sprint. Not only do they run like the wind, but they can hop ten, twenty lengths at a time once they get rolling, and where they go is totally unpredictable. That's why they're so difficult—impossible, really—to catch without the element of surprise.

It's-ə not-ə unpredictable.

That got my tail going.

He cozied up close, crazy jack, and told me there was a logic to the way hares escape. At first, I didn't believe him because, how could that be? If you've ever watched one, you know what I mean.

He insisted there was a pattern, or more accurately a series of patterns, and he'd be willing to share them with me in return for an iron-clad guarantee of safety. Fine with me, but wasn't he concerned about the ramifications? He was, after all, sharing a survival secret of his whole species with the top of the food chain.

Who yə gonna tell-ə?

A fair question. I might have said, "My kids," but his point was made. And because I wasn't so fond of jack meat anyway, the whole thing was low risk for him.

But what was *I* getting out of it?

Yv be the only-ə killer in history who know-ə.

They say rabbits have a way with words, but I'll take harespeak any day.

He started drawing in the dirt, using pebbles to mark takeoff and landing spots, explaining how, if he's here, then he goes there, unless... and so on. Next, he went through a series of variables—terrain, weather, time of day—but rather than going into more detail, suffice it to say, he was making sense.

Seeing it laid out on the ground was one thing, but trying to follow in live action would be another. He'd anticipated my doubts and suggested we go through the motions, slowly to start, then speeding up, little by little.

Sounded like a fine idea.

I was astonished to learn the answer to the question I'd always asked myself: How do they decide where to go next, when they're moving so fast? The answer was, they already know, even before they land. Because it's a pattern. Not recognizable to anyone but them. And now, me.

We went through it a dozen times, faster each round. Twice I noticed spectators, a coatimundi and a skunk, and glanced over to scare them off. Not that they would've figured out what we were doing, but I assumed Lazarus didn't want to risk it. Besides, I don't like being watched. *I'm* supposed to be the voyeur around here. (I imagine a few birds could see, but with their tiny brains, who cares?)

When we made it through the whole progression at full speed, Lazarus said, *Now yə know-ə.*

And I did. But I was curious; would it be the same in a real-life situation?

He recommended I go chase a hare, but I didn't care enough to do that. I just wanted to know. Either he'd given me the secrets or he hadn't.

Then he told me his idea, which, in retrospect, he'd probably come up with beforehand. *How about-ə I bring-ə Jɛəricho. Yə can try on-ə him.*

Excellent. Jericho was one of the fastest, most coordinated animals on earth. If I could catch him, I could catch them all.

The next day, Lazarus returned, this time with Jericho. An impressive specimen he was, slightly taller and heavier than Lazarus, all muscle and sinew. I thought to myself, he wouldn't be tasty at all. Then I decided to say it out loud, in hopes of getting Jericho to relax. It had the opposite effect, unfortunately, and Jericho wanted to leave, but Lazarus calmed him with his silver tongue.

Yə safety be guaranteed-ə. Guaranteed-ə!

Jericho said, *Let's-ə get it over with-ə,* and took off.

I launched after him.

Lazarus had taught me well. I knew where Jericho was going, it seemed, before he did. He kept looking back as if to say, how are you doing this? And I smelled fear.

There was nothing to be afraid of—I wasn't going to eat him—but I suppose he couldn't have known that for sure, so he switched into higher gear.

I stayed right with him.

He was soaring twenty-five, thirty lengths per leap, in what seemed to be random directions, and I was practically waiting for him each time he landed. His movements took on an urgency, like he was losing control. I'd seen this kind of wildness before.

I knew right away from the cracking sound as Jericho crumpled into a careening ball of ears, fur, and dust. He'd landed on a rabbit hole in just the wrong way—a freak accident—and broken a hind leg. He stared at me in shock as Lazarus rushed over.

Shiny bone was sticking out of Jericho's thigh, and blood rushing from the jagged wound had already drained the color from his face.

I'm-ə doomed, he said.

Lazarus disagreed with vehemence, saying no, that wasn't true, he'd be fine, he only needed time to recover, and besides, *Yə has-ə the protection-ə.* Lazarus checked me for agreement, and I mouthed a yes.

In all cases, a broken limb in the desert is a death sentence, even for the King. Jericho knew that. Lazarus knew that. Everybody knows that.

Lazarus wouldn't give up, reminding Jericho that with my pledge, he could live out his life in peace and certainty.

Jericho tried to sit up, but couldn't. *Not-ə runnin an jumpin, no-ə.* Lying on his back, he looked at me and pointed to his neck. *Please-ə.*

Lazarus said, *No-ə! Yə don need-ə! Please-ə!*

One was begging me to do what the other was begging me not to. I looked at both jacks, flicked a paw, and it was over. Jericho was gone.

After a long time, Lazarus spoke. *I guess yə did him a favor-ə.*

I swished my tail and nodded.

Would yə eat him-ə? Keep him from-ə the buzzards-ə?

I said of course, as soon as he left, and it was the least I could do.

Lazarus asked that we forget the whole thing, meaning he'd receive nothing from me, and there would be no more lessons. (Not that I needed them.) I suppose he didn't want the story to get out, but he wasn't thinking straight; he should've known he'd get blamed anyway. In retrospect, I don't know which bothered him more (or was it less?), the death of his friend or the loss of our deal.

I haven't spoken with him since, but I've seen him a few times from a distance. He's still remarkable, and now he's got a new partner, his son—a hybrid, they say. I don't know what it means, but I'll find out soon enough. There really are no secrets out here. ♦

REDS, PART I
THE SOW WHO LOVED ME

The man and his dog came from downwind. Rufus, the youngest collared peccary in the herd, was closest, and the first to become aware. He'd never smelled anything like it, but knew it was dangerous, and started squalling just before the alien beast started barking. The ruckus alerted Rufus's mother, Ruby. Scenting the threat she clacked her teeth, released an odor of alarm, and took off. Carmine was next to flee, then the rest: Rowan, Scarlett, Blaze, and Russell, all in different directions.

Rufus ran and ran, his two-month-old legs stumbling over rocks and roots. He stopped to listen. Nothing. But the air was still full of fear, so he kept on, until exhaustion made him quit. He stood in a wash that looked, to his myopic eyes, like the one they'd wandered through an hour before, but it didn't smell right. He squalled again, this time for his mother.

The wind shifted and he knew the dog was on him. Backed up against a high bank, Rufus was trapped. The dog had escaped its owner and was pointing and baying. From his left, Rufus smelled kinship. It wasn't his mother, but the aroma of defensive aggression combined with the sound of three adult peccaries attacking the overmatched pet (who yelped in retreat with a gash to the foreleg) felt like divine intervention.

Rufus stood stiff-legged while the adults—two boars and a sow—surrounded him. Their dorsal bristles erect from the conflict, they appeared twice their normal size, and their scents were familiar only to a point, after which Rufus knew these peccaries were not part of his family. His knees quaked at the sow's approach, until she nuzzled his neck as his mother had always done. She slid her head down his body to his nipplelike scent gland, just above his tiny tail, which she rubbed with her face and neck. She lowered her own gland enough for him to reach, and he rubbed back.[1]

She understood he'd been abandoned and offered to adopt him, if he was willing. His gland expressed that he had no other options and was thankful to have been saved from the slobbering menace. The sow reversed direction and put her cheek against Rufus's nose so he could familiarize himself with the collective perfume of his new clan. He detected standoffishness from one of the boars and disinterest from the other, and although he wasn't sure which was which, he was heartened that neither was giving off even a whiff of aggression toward *him*.

Staying within nuzzling range of Katya, Rufus followed his guardians over a ridge and into a valley full of similar smells. When they reached the group, everyone introduced themselves *peccary style*: reciprocal rubbing of faces on scent glands. Within minutes, all the scent Rufus had carried from his prior association, including that of his mother, was masked over.

There were Boris and Anton, the two boars Katya had been out with; a younger male named Misha; and two more sows, Olga and Ludmilla. Olga had twin females roughly Rufus's age, Vanya and Irina.

Still skittish, Rufus felt most comfortable near the warm, friendly scent of Katya, but he was hungry, and she wasn't nursing. She led him to Olga, who put her snout in the air. Katya let Rufus know he should stand apart for a moment, which he did, while the sows argued. Things got heated, with Olga resisting whatever Katya was requesting. Anton came over to put added pressure on Olga, who finally lay down and lifted a leg. When her own offspring tried to suckle, she pushed them away. Rufus, now ravenous, went to the recumbent sow, dropped flat on his belly, and as soon as he felt her raised leg on the top of his head,

---

1   These and other collared peccary behaviors were observed and described by Raymond Eugene Schweinsburg (1969).

Rachel Ivanyi

grabbed a long nipple and suckled as he was born to do. Olga's glandular expression and vocalizations went from aggravated to contented. After Rufus had his fill, he moved off, making space for the twins.

This wasn't so bad.

Until the middle of the night, when Rufus discovered genuine chill as he huddled with the group. Was this narrow overhang their only protection from the cold? He expressed his feelings. Katya's reassurance was soothing, but more so was the general consensus—a reeking confidence—that their shelter predicament was *temporary*. With fresh faith and a full belly, Rufus slept, his mother's memory already half-faded.

As the months passed, temperatures rose to where staying warm at night was less of a challenge than avoiding the sun. The peccaries adjusted their schedule accordingly, walking the territory and feeding after dark. During the day, Rufus felt like he'd shrivel to nothing if he wasn't in the shade and constantly hydrating, which in itself was difficult, until the summer's first significant rain.

And how glorious it was, except for the spot of hail and a thunderclap that dispersed the herd. This time, though, Katya had found the terrified Rufus soon after, and he could tell from her musk that unlike his birth mother, Katya would always come back for him. He fell deep in love with his adoptive parent and resolved to stay with her as long as he lived. He played with Vanya and Irina that summer, too, in the middle of the night, the only time cool enough for frolic. They accepted him like a brother, and he grew fond of them.

Katya and Ludmilla gave birth to small litters in the fall farrowing season, but of the four babies, two died at birth and one was taken by an owl the first week. Boris was more upset than anyone, accusing the sows, without being specific, of negligence (a claim Rufus didn't understand, because Boris had never paid any attention to him or the twins).

The lone survivor, Dmitri, was Katya's, but she abdicated her parental duties to Ludmilla, who was overflowing with milk.

When spring came again, the twins exuded a different kind of affection. They wanted something from Rufus, but weren't sure how to express their desire. It didn't help that Rufus was much more interested *that way* in Katya than he was in the females his own age. Day after day, night after night, he watched Katya sleep between Boris and Anton, their three bodies touching. Sometimes it was after she'd been mounted (by Boris, never by Anton), sometimes not, but always, their combined odor triggered in Rufus a mix of fear, aggression, desire, and jealousy. How could Anton possibly abide?

The lack of sleep was starting to wear on Rufus, and he could think of only one solution. When Boris and Anton were distracted, quarreling over a dead pack rat, Rufus approached Katya, and as they rubbed, he made his amorous intentions known. Katya darted away and clacked her teeth in warning, which brought Boris and Anton running. Anton stood back, but Boris went straight to Rufus with nose up and javelin teeth bared. Katya's rebuff had already cooled Rufus's ardor, and he was in no mood to fight with their unquestioned leader. Rufus lay flat, a sign of total submission. Boris rubbed his neck along Rufus's gland, letting Rufus know: if he ever tried to mount Katya again, he'd regret it. Boris walked off nonchalantly, reinforcing his dominance.

Katya's reluctance notwithstanding, Rufus had detected something from Katya, he was sure—a desire to mate with *him*. But she'd tried to hide it. Why? Had Boris detected it also? If not, perhaps someone should enlighten him. Rufus raised his hind quarters to a moderate defensive position and released an odor of defiance. Boris wheeled around in a clacking, growling rage, ready to charge.

Katya ran to Boris, backing her genitals and anus up to his nose in an attempt to distract. Boris's pale penis extended from its sheath, but he pushed Katya away with his huge head. His clacking got faster and louder, and he scraped at the dirt. Rufus, still with his front hooves and head low to the ground, clacked and growled back.

Afraid of an ensuing clash, Katya approached Boris from behind, turned her head sideways, and began licking the corkscrew tip of his dangling organ. At the same time, she released her most fetching odor, and the irresistible combination of stimuli was enough to make Boris forget about Rufus and turn his attention to the comely sow, whose stench in that moment could have filled three valleys.

Katya led Boris away, and although Rufus knew what was happening, he stayed put. What he'd received from Katya in the exchange—that she shared his desire—was life altering, and he began to consider how he might exploit it. (He was a child no longer.)

Anton, always coolheaded and diplomatic, was chosen the next day to deliver the message, more of a demand than a request. Because of Rufus's offense in presuming to mate with Katya, he now had to prove his loyalty by infiltrating the neighboring clan that included his mother. He was to gather intelligence about their leadership, movements, and defenses, as well as evaluate their strengths and weaknesses.

The half-square-mile area occupied by Carmine's group was relatively small and unimpressive, except for one thing: an old mine shaft that provided excellent protection from temporal extremes. With reliable information and the element of surprise, Boris's group, larger and physically stronger en masse, should be able to capture enough territory to take over the shaft. They'd never sleep in the freezing cold again.

To make the demand more attractive, Anton expressed in no uncertain terms that should Rufus agree to the mission, and should it prove successful, he'd have unlimited access to Katya in whatever way he chose. Then, with a hint of belligerence, Anton laid out two options: accept and leave at once, without speaking to Katya or anyone else; or, be viciously attacked by Boris and Anton and Misha.

Rufus wasn't afraid of Boris or anybody else, but he understood the concept of being outnumbered, and the prospect of mounting Katya whenever he wanted was so appealing that he agreed.

He remembered his mother's name, but couldn't recall her scent.

Would Ruby remember him? ♦

REDS, PART II
THE PECCARY WHO CAME IN FROM THE COLD

In his one and a half years, Rufus had never even thought about traveling alone.

He could start the journey right away or find somewhere to rest until dark. He chose the former, because he'd never heard coyotes hunting in packs during the day.

It helped that he was already so close to the territorial boundary. Of course—Boris had *steered* them here because he'd been planning this for a long time. How long? From the beginning? The day baby Rufus, lost and alone, wandered into the domain of his family's bitter rivals? Had Boris decided right then to raise an adopted son as a weapon of war?

It didn't matter. Boris and the rest of them knew (and Rufus was glad they knew) Rufus cared about only one thing—Katya. If he had to go and learn about the neighbors, so be it. They were his birth family after all.

He found a north–south deer path and followed it past rocks and cactuses and shrubbery and an occasional tree. The sun was approaching the top of the ridge when the smells changed. The comfort of familiarity became the disquiet of the unknown, except it wasn't only unknown, it was the enemy—the slovenly, uncivilized pigs[1] to the north.

He noticed patterned scrapes in the dirt. Looking around, he found more on a palo verde tree, then on another. The markings of a defended territory. He'd crossed the border. His salt-and-pepper bristles stood at

---

1   a grave insult

moderate attention. He was trespassing and the occupants could appear any moment.

His eyes weren't good enough to use sight cues for navigation (no peccary's are), but Anton's instructions had been easy to follow: Cut straight across the eastern slope of the mountain, not gaining or losing elevation, to the wire fence. Turn west and follow the fence until it turns north. From there, go up the rise to the mine shaft.

Rufus gathered his thoughts before the final climb. He considered how he might act at first contact. The obvious (and simplest) approach was an attitude of pure passivity. He was only one against a herd of how many? Six to eight, Anton had said.

Another option was hyperaggression. When it had first occurred to him, he'd dismissed it, but the more he deliberated, the more sense it made. The hard part was making the hostility believable. What if he ran in woofing and gnashing and they ignored him? They wouldn't do that, would they?

He tried to find—manufacture—ill will toward his parents, but failed. He felt no resentment over his abandonment, because he'd met Katya as a result. (On the best day of his life!) His ire would have to be directed at Boris—because Boris didn't care about anyone but Boris. And in the process, Boris controlled and mistreated everyone.

Nearing his destination, Rufus felt the wind at his back. They'd smell him before they saw him. Good. He was going to make noise anyway, because the last thing he wanted was to sneak up on them. One or more might panic and do something dangerous.

He heard woofing and knew he'd been detected. It was farther than he could see, but he guessed from the sound it was less than thirty body lengths. He took off running and clacking. Now he wished the wind was in his face, because he'd have a better idea of what he was running into. It sounded like three adults. He kept sprinting, with a plan to go until he reached the back of the mine shaft or somebody made him stop. To make himself angry, he pictured Boris mounting Katya. Then he imagined Katya resisting, and Boris overpowering her.

Suddenly, all he could see was prickly pear. What? He stopped and went silent. Prickly pear was one of the most common plants in the desert, scattered across all elevations and soil types, but *this* patch was unlike any other. The cacti were low but packed together in a wide swath and extending out in both directions like...a *barricade*. The woofing continued from beyond the green. How was he supposed to get near the shaft if the area was blocked off?

He picked a direction and trotted along the cacti. He could hear peccaries tracking him along the inside. When he reached an opening, the wind changed. He smelled the three adults at the same time as he saw them. They stood in a tight line at the entrance. Rufus recommitted himself to the aggressive tactic and charged, clacking his teeth as loud and fast as he could.

Two boars and a sow stood their ground as Rufus sped forward. When he realized they weren't going to move (and he was going to barrel into them), he skidded to a stop. They were quiet and their bristles lay flat. Exactly the sort of reaction he'd been afraid of.

These purported enemies didn't seem the least bit alarmed by his presence. They knew he was angry, frightened, and confused, which he was, although not for the reasons they might have thought. They made it clear to him they were secure and *able to defend themselves*. Rufus had expected confidence, but not to this degree.

The sow stepped forward. Was it Ruby? Rufus relaxed his bristles as she came alongside. She offered a mutual rubbing of musk glands and he accepted. With his nose right on her, he was sure: *his mother*, his very first smell, which he'd forgotten until now. She remembered him too,

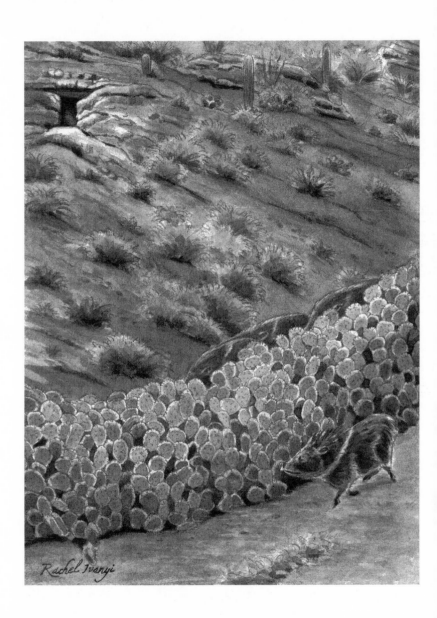

and her scent profile went from welcoming to affectionate. Rufus was surprised by the intensity of her feelings.

Carmine approached with his snout held level (not raised). This too was unusual, because Carmine *was* the group's dominant male. Or was he? Had he been supplanted? No, the scent coming from Carmine was pure dominance, but of a quiet variety, not the in-your-face obnoxiousness of Boris.

Rufus's first interaction with these peccaries had thrown him completely off balance. And what was going on with the prickly pear?

Ruby's apologies for losing Rufus felt genuine. She'd heard him and searched, but he'd already wandered too far into enemy territory, and because the herd had scattered, she had no help. She'd hoped all this time he'd been adopted, because getting raised by the luddites to the south was infinitely better than getting eaten before one's first birthday.

Rufus was ready for the question when asked: why are you here? He detailed in malodorous terms Boris's offenses and deficiencies. Boris and he had fought over a sow, too, and one of them *needed to go*. (Rufus had decided on partial truth as the most believable explanation.) Ruby expressed an interest in the sow—Katya, right?—but it evaporated after a moment.

The spring nights weren't cold, but when Rufus saw the mine shaft[2] he understood right away how valuable it was as a shelter. Plus: it held runoff for weeks after a rain, so these lucky peccaries had a private water supply part of the time. (Shared watering holes led to squabbles and fights and were frequented by predators.)

---

2   a horizontal tunnel going into the side of a hill

There were six adults—Carmine, Ruby, boars Russell and Rowan, and sows Scarlett and Blaze. The two youngsters, Rose and Ginger, were no longer *reds*[3] but weren't quite mature (old enough to fight and mate).

Rufus noticed that Rowan was slow-moving and less engaged than the others. Rufus didn't ask about it, but gathered through communication going on around him that the old peccary was ill and might be leaving soon. Sensing Rufus's concern, Ruby gave an upbeat explanation of how Rowan's struggles to keep up during grazing was what gave her the idea of *growing their own food* in the first place.

She'd observed what happened when a segment of prickly pear was left on the ground: it took root and spread quickly. Rather than asking Rowan to suffer through the miles of daily foraging, Ruby brought back paddles. Some she gave to him and some she half-buried. The peccaries were disciplined about not eating the new growth, and before long, her gardening yielded the largest prickly pear patch anyone had ever seen. Right next to their home base![4]

(Later, on his way back to meet Anton, Rufus would figure out why they'd never made this discovery in *his* territory: Boris was a neat freak. Each grazing area had to be clear of ground debris before they moved on, and no half-eaten paddles were to be left on the plants. If the herd was scattered mid-meal, they went back to clean up later.)

It was also Ruby who'd thought of using cactus for protection. To Rufus it made so much sense! And in hindsight, what had taken them so long? Even pack rats knew how to employ spines against predators.

Rufus was amazed. Contrary to what he'd been told, these peccaries were polite, considerate, intelligent, creative, and, most of all, friendly. He assumed he'd misunderstood the first time Carmine offered

---

3 Young peccaries are called reds because of their reddish color, which lasts until around two months of age.

4 Rufus was gone before he was old enough to notice.

up Scarlett or Blaze for mounting. Really? Boris would never do that—*share*, just because. In contrast to Boris's nastiness and intimidation, Carmine managed to maintain order with open-mindedness and tolerance.

Rufus couldn't understand why his adoptive family would have lied so much about his birth parents, until he realized it was pure ignorance. The "hippies over yonder" had discovered agriculture, and nobody in Boris's group had any inkling. Ruby indicated it was because Boris didn't do his homework and thought he knew everything. Not bothering to keep close watch over his enemies, he was content with waiting for the population numbers to swing in his favor. Plus—Rufus and Ruby grasped this at the same time—Boris had been waiting for Rufus to grow up.

Boris was going to know everything soon, though, because Rufus was going to tell him. And when Boris learned about the fortifications around the mine shaft, he'd give up on invading. It was *never going to happen*. (But learning how to grow food and upgrade security at the home base should ease the pain of a few dozen subfreezing nights per year.)

Rufus was supposed to meet Anton at the boundary on day six (in the early afternoon, at moonrise) to give his first report. Sneaking off wouldn't be difficult, because unlike Boris, Carmine didn't keep tabs on everyone. Rufus had mixed emotions, though, about continuing his espionage. While he was still obsessed with and would do anything for Katya, he felt a sincere (and unexpected) affection for his birth family, and Ruby in particular.

Ruby again surprised him when she shared what she *already knew*: Rufus was a spy. And it didn't bother her. She was only glad and grateful to see him alive.

Rufus wanted reassurance. She'd really searched for him, that awful day? Tried her hardest?

Yes, yes, yes, she insisted. She'd tried, but when she'd heard the dog getting attacked, all she could do was hope. Her scent was powerful and pure, and Rufus believed her.

She went on to encourage him: Go tell them everything! That our defenses are impenetrable! Share what we've learned, and our vision of a better tomorrow! With a predictable, sustainable food and water[5] supply, she argued, there'd be no need for territories or boundaries. Because if everyone had enough, there'd be nothing to fight over.

Rufus was intrigued by the concept and wanted to know if anyone was going to be in charge. After some evasiveness, Ruby let it slip that she and Carmine might *have* to be in charge, because peccaries like Boris, stuck in the past, were an ongoing threat to any new peace. Rufus showed consternation, and she backpedaled. Nobody would be in charge, she asserted, because *why?* If there was no need? She changed the subject, making sure Rufus knew he was welcome to stay, or leave and come back, or whatever he'd like. As her child, he'd always have a place in the family.

Rufus appreciated her openness and generosity.

One thing Ruby *wasn't* candid about: she believed no matter what Rufus told Boris, the old warmonger would want to attack anyway. (And they'd be ready.)

Rufus had a lot to think about as he strode back to the border. Anton was there, but Rufus didn't stop to visit. He kept going, with Anton following, to where the group was grazing next to their winter overhang. Rufus was prepared to tell Boris everything, but first he wanted to smell Katya.

Boris ran out to meet him. (No Katya yet!) They walked off, just the two of them. Rufus described an unusual few days with his ex-family, noting they were different from what he'd expected. Not only had

---

5   Desert peccaries meet most of their hydration needs by eating cactus.

they learned how to grow food, they'd used cactus to turn the mine shaft into a fortress. The invasion idea should be scrapped, because it was guaranteed to fail. (Rufus left out the part about the peccaries all coming together in one big happy group, knowing Boris wouldn't see the potential of it.)

Rufus dug a short trench with his snout and trotted over to a nearby prickly pear. He chewed off a paddle and brought it back. He showed Boris how to set it in the trench and cover the bottom with dirt, which really shouldn't happen until *after* the cutting wound had scabbed over. Boris didn't understand. Rufus was getting frustrated. The process was simple, but Boris wasn't paying close enough attention.

Then Rufus found out why. Boris didn't care about growing cactus, or fortifications, or most of all how Rufus felt about his mother. All Boris could think about was the mine shaft. He wanted that territory, no matter the cost. And he had a plan.

Rufus had stopped paying attention too. He wanted Katya, *at last.* Where was she?

Boris growled at the suggestion. Anton and Misha came over. Rufus reacted defensively, dropping to one knee and growling back. He'd done what'd been asked. All of it. What more did they want?

Boris clarified: Rufus could have unlimited time with Katya *after* the invasion.

Invasion? He must be crazy.

Rufus was waiting for Anton or Misha to offer a different opinion, but as usual, they wouldn't disagree with Boris. Not even a little. They were all crazy! If they wanted to follow their deranged leader to doom, they could, but they'd have to do it without Rufus. Or Katya. Katya wouldn't be involved in something like this, Rufus was sure. She was too smart. Was that why she wasn't there now? Had she already left?

No—she'd come up behind him, from downwind, and he had no idea. She walked past without turning her head.

Katya?

His heart swelled and cracked at the same time.

She didn't look at him until she was standing shoulder to shoulder with Boris. She expressed unqualified support for Boris's decision, adding that, if Rufus wanted to remain a part of the family, he needed to participate.

Rufus was stunned. Boris commanded them all to rest up, because they were leaving that night. The pigs to the north would never expect an attack so soon. ♦

REDS, PART III
HERD WAR

Pigs* to the North			Luddites to the South		
Males					
Carmine	6 years	57 lb	Boris	8 years	62 lb
Russell	4 years	51 lb	Misha	5 years	49 lb
Rowan**	12 years	46 lb	Rufus	19 months	47 lb
			Anton	6 years	45 lb
			Dmitri	10 months	39 lb
Females					
Ruby	6 years	46 lb	Olga	9 years	50 lb
Scarlett	6 years	41 lb	Katya	6 years	41 lb
Blaze	4 years	39 lb	Ludmilla	4 years	38 lb
Rose	7 months	22 lb	Vanya	18 months	34 lb
Ginger	7 months	19 lb	Irina	18 months	32 lb

* Collared peccaries, also called javelinas, are not pigs.

** Infirm

Besides being more aggressive by nature (except when females are protecting their own very young children), adult *Tayassu tajaku*[1] males outweigh females and have thicker, longer teeth. With five full-grown boars against the Pigs' three (one of whom was infirm), the Luddites had a clear advantage. So too with the females: five to three in favor of the Luddites, because the youngest Pigs, Rose and Ginger, were still juveniles. Under normal circumstances, on neutral territory, the Luddites would wipe the Pigs off the field.

This was not neutral territory, and these were not normal circumstances.

The battlefield was inside the Pigs' boundary, giving them a home-turf advantage. Also, they'd spent years figuring out how to defend themselves with subterfuge, misdirection, and prickly pear.

Boris had already known what his enemies were up to, and the more he learned, the less he cared. He had no need for fancy strategies and scenarios. Overwhelming force was simple, beautiful, and indefensible.

He'd forbidden Rufus to share his knowledge with the others. When Rufus *was* finally allowed to greet Katya, he expressed only love, lust, and confusion. Why was she acting cold to him? Had he not done what'd been asked? What more would it take for her to reciprocate? Was it even possible? Her unresponsiveness was driving him insane. Had he been able to make a connection—any at all—he'd have urged her to sneak off right then. (Both of them switching sides might tip the scales of war.)

If only she could see how beautiful their life could be.

Not responding had taken all of Katya's strength. She *did* want to reciprocate, but was afraid of Boris finding out. And if she left, like she had once before, Boris would stop at nothing to get her back. (The Bandits to the West, who'd abetted her defection, had paid dearly in the

---

1   collared peccary

form of slain children.) Being with Rufus, she knew, was going to happen only over Boris's murdered body.

Katya couldn't risk sharing her intention with Rufus. Because he wasn't mature enough to control his emotions, he might reveal her secret, dooming them both.

00:22 Mountain Standard Time. The team followed Boris in single file, alternating male and female. They trudged over the ground with muted harumphing until they reached the end of the fence at the foot of the last rise. Boris wanted to verify something Rufus had reported—that there was only one way in and out of the enclosure. Boris exchanged scents with Misha, who trotted northwest, up the hill but at an angle.

The light of the half-moon was not enough, and Misha trotted straight into the wall of prickly pear north of the opening. He didn't hear anything. Why not? They should have detected him by now; the breeze was at his back. As instructed, he walked the perimeter counterclockwise, rubbing up against the cactus, feeling for breaks. He spent almost an hour going around. Boris had told him to be sure.

02:31 MST. The intelligence confirmed, Boris gave the order, and the army of ten walked—not ran—toward the enemy. They didn't clack, growl, or woof. And there was no piloerection[2] (which wouldn't have mattered anyway in the dark). The intimidation would come later. They stopped advancing once each side had detected the scent of the other.

Carmine and Russell stood abreast at the entrance. They weren't vocalizing either. They were as calm and quiet as when Rufus had appeared out of nowhere the week before.

Anton approached Carmine. They stood cheek to cheek and slid their faces down each other's body. With his usual coolness, Anton delivered the message from Boris: *surrender or die.*

Carmine made it clear that surrender was not an option.

---

2   stiffening of hair and bristles

Anton had expected this, and tried appealing to Carmine's sense of reason. Carmine was outnumbered, ten to six. It wasn't a fair fight. Resistance was suicide.

Carmine resisted.

With nonchalance, Anton elaborated: Boris would kill every one of them if he had to take the mine shaft by force. Whereas, if they left now, they could keep *most* of their territory.

Carmine resisted.

Anton expressed genuine regret before turning away.

Carmine knew Boris would send three boars to begin. It didn't matter that Carmine and Russell were big and strong and ferocious and desperate. Against three, the best they could achieve was a draw. The second wave would be two more males and all five sows against old Rowan, three sows, and the two youngsters. Anyone surviving the assault would be trapped in the compound and executed. (The young females might be spared, if Boris found them pleasing enough.)

Rufus's mind raced. Would he be called on to fight? What would he do? Compared to Katya his birth family meant nothing, but he didn't want them dead, either. The violence was senseless. If only Carmine would concede!

Rufus didn't have to make a decision yet, because Boris picked Anton, Misha, and Dmitri (only ten months old and underweight but fast and nimble) to charge first. Once Carmine and Russell were defeated, Boris could clean up the rest, alone if need be. Rufus might not have to fight at all.

Carmine and Ruby had other plans, of course.

03:06 MST. Carmine and Russell were ready to meet the first wave. Ruby and Scarlett stood off to the side. Rose and Ginger were hiding in the mine shaft, the entrance concealed with vegetation. Blaze was crouched higher on the hill, above another tunnel. (The miners' first attempt had an unstable ceiling, so they moved a few yards and started again. Overgrown by weeds and vines, the original dig sat undiscovered for decades, until Ruby found it by accident.)

At the top of the cactus corral, Rowan was ready to slip out the back when the fighting started, through a narrow gap Misha had missed in spite of his best effort.

Twenty feet from Carmine and Russell, Anton, Misha, and Dmitri pawed the dirt. Behind them were Boris and Rufus. The five sows stood in the rear, hoping not to be called on.

All was quiet until Boris gave the order.

The three boars charged open-mouthed, teeth pointed to the front like cocked spears. Carmine and Russell stood their ground, noses up and ears forward. The attackers collided with the defenders and everyone fell down.

They were five peccaries in a space for three. They stood on their hind legs, roaring and biting at faces. It was hard to tell who was who, but within a few exchanges, Misha and Anton had latched onto both sides of Carmine's neck. They shook their heads back and forth, sinking their fangs deeper.

Just outside the fort, Russell and Dmitri were similarly joined. Having a weight advantage, Russell whirled the pair in circles and performed a textbook throw down. Dimitri was defeated, but didn't let go. Nothing could make him let go. His only job was to keep Russell occupied, and thinking of Ludmilla made it easy. She'd suckled him (past the normal weaning age, because it had pleased them both), raised him, guided him, loved him. And though Ludmilla wasn't his mother, Dmitri was as attached to her as Rufus was to Katya. (Neither situation was an accident, but part of how Boris kept control of the herd.)

Anton let go and slid farther down Carmine's side. While Misha held on at the neck, Anton bit at Carmine's back and rump, piercing the

scent gland and causing an involuntary squirt of musk. Carmine was tired and close to defeat. Ruby and Scarlett stood and watched, powerless. If they tried to help, Boris would send in the next wave.

For twenty minutes, Misha and Carmine stayed locked in their bloody embrace, first standing, then sitting, then lying down. Anton never stopped biting. Carmine's stony occipital ridge and thick fur had protected him from serious damage to the neck and head, but what was happening on his hind end was another story. Even if the assault had ceased right then, he wouldn't have survived the dozens of puncture wounds.

When Anton was certain Carmine was no longer a threat, he clacked six times, slow and loud. Boris heard, and was pleased. He'd been almost sure he'd need reinforcements for disabling Carmine, but no. His three warriors had been enough.

04:11 MST. Boris was about to go in when he detected something. From over his right shoulder.

One of the sows was expressing alarm.

Now all of them were expressing alarm.

A clacking male. Flank attack!

Just what Boris had been afraid of, which was why, when he'd sent Misha to check for exits, he'd had Dimitri sniff the area for peccaries lying in wait.

More than anything, Boris was irritated. He ordered Rufus to follow. They were going to engage whoever was attacking from the rear. It couldn't be serious, because the only legitimate threats, Carmine and Russell, had already been neutralized. Whatever this was shouldn't take long.

Back at the corral, Ruby and Scarlett didn't need long. Scarlett attacked Anton with the ferocity of a mother protecting her newborn young. He outweighed her by five pounds, but she managed to get her teeth in his neck and hold on. Despite being thrown down, she didn't let go. At the same time, Ruby bit the exhausted Misha on the ears until he released Carmine, who was too wounded to stand, or even kneel.

Carmine started dragging himself by his forelegs toward the shaft beneath Blaze. He needed to get inside.

Boris and Rufus reached the sows and found only Rowan. He'd been subdued by Olga and wasn't resisting. *This* was the flank attack? A diversion!

Boris was enraged, though another few minutes weren't going to matter. He opened his mouth as wide as it would go and closed it around Rowan's grayed face, fangs piercing both eye sockets. Rowan convulsed once before dying.

The taste of blood. Boris had it now. He wheeled around. Finally!

Rufus inhaled something more pungent than the smell of war—the smell of *no mercy*. Boris went to his sows, one by one. It was time to claim their new home.

Katya was still avoiding Rufus. Why?

04:41 MST. The seven of them—Boris, Rufus, Olga, Katya, Ludmilla, Vanya, and Irina—stepped past Russell and Dmitri at the corral's opening. Seeing Ludmilla gave Dmitri renewed strength and he reinforced his bite, causing Russell to groan.

Inside was Misha, who was down but recovering. Then there were Anton and Scarlett; Anton had her pinned, but she still wouldn't release him. She did when Boris bit down hard on her back foot, breaking a half-dozen bones and causing her to evacuate her bladder and bowels.

Next Boris stood in front of the crawling Carmine. Boris basked in the aroma of triumph, mocking his rival. Here everyone! Here lies the mighty Carmine at my feet! Insult after insult emanated from Boris's gland.

Carmine kept trying, bumping his head on Boris's knees.

Rufus had done nothing, yet he felt responsible for what had happened and—worse—what was about to happen. He approached Katya. Yet again she rebuffed him. Making him crazy! What was she doing? She loved him, didn't she? As much as he loved her! He'd felt it, that day! So why, now, was she so cold?

Katya was waiting for her chance. She was almost out of time.

04:51 MST. Boris didn't need to deliver a fatal blow to Carmine. He was already dead.

04:52 MST. Ruby came alongside Katya and shared the plan. It was risky, confiding in the enemy, but this particular enemy was in love with her son. (Ruby had challenged Rufus during his stay: Was he *sure* Katya felt the same? He'd been sure. Surer than he'd ever been of anything.)

04:54 MST. Katya clacked to get everyone's attention. Ruby was devastated, believing she'd made a fatal error in judgment, until Katya started releasing vicious insults—bitter, spiteful, and condescending—at Boris. Both sides were confused. What was Katya doing?

Boris wasn't confused. He'd had enough willfulness from this sow over the years, and though he'd been fond of her once, as fond as he could be of anyone, she'd become too much trouble. Besides, he was about to acquire a pair of young females. One if not both could take Katya's place. He stood on his hind legs and brought his front hooves down on Katya's head, trying to knock her out. She was dazed, but didn't fall.

Rufus smelled Katya's pain and charged Boris.

Ruby crashed into Rufus from the side, knocking him down. What? Why? Rufus was frenzied, trying to get free, but his mother had clamped onto his hind leg.

Katya ran from Boris up the slope to the tunnel, entering the pitch black. How far back did it go? Not very. In a few paces she reached the end. She turned to face him.

Boris thought there was something off about the mine shaft, but couldn't identify what. He'd figure it out right after silencing Katya, who was still spewing disrespect. After all he'd done for her!

Katya heard Rufus woofing. He'd gotten free from his mother and was coming to save her. Oh no! Don't! Stay away!

Ruby was clacking. Was that the signal to Blaze? Katya didn't want Rufus to die. Hurry, Blaze! Do it now!

Blaze pulled a stick from under a boulder, sending ten tons of dirt and rocks down over the entry to the bogus shaft. Boris and Katya were sealed inside.

05:06 MST. Dust covered everyone and everything. Rufus was digging with his nose, then his front feet. Ruby tried to comfort him, but he shoved her away. He needed to save Katya. What had happened? Why weren't they helping? He dug and dug. He wasn't making any progress.

Ruby left him alone, as did the others. They cleared the brush from the front of the real shaft, and Rose and Ginger came out. Rowan's body was retrieved and laid by Carmine's.

(Collapsing the tunnel had been Ruby's idea. Plan A was to get Boris in alone and plan B was for Carmine to lure him. When neither came to pass, Ruby had gambled on Katya.)

Without their commander, the Luddites had no interest in continuing the fight. They left for home drained and defeated as the sun appeared over the hills. Rufus was not with them.

A week later, Rufus's grief had abated enough for him to eat and walk around. Ruby asked him to deliver a message to his adoptive group: they were welcome to join. Boars, sows, everyone. Any lingering resentment would be directed at Boris only. The Luddites would join their new family as equals.

They soon combined to make a herd of fourteen. While there was no official leader, Ruby was the one they all looked to for guidance when needed. At her urging, they shared their technology with any peccary who asked. Through absorption, adoption, and years of successful breeding, the Pigs to the North (who were actually peccaries of the Southwest) became one of the largest herds in the history of the New World, numbering over a hundred.

They should've numbered fifteen at the merger, but Rufus couldn't stay. Not with Katya's body right there.

Where would he go? How would he survive alone?

He'd never be alone, because Katya's soul was with him.

Before leaving, he'd thanked his mother, using no uncertain terms. ♦

FRENCH KISSING
FOR BEGINNERS

The day before, Gil had enjoyed his second meal of the year (it wasn't quite May), and many of the calories from the dozen quail eggs and four newborn rabbits had already gone to storage in his tail. His bladder was three-quarters full too, which meant he could go another fifty days before his next drink.

Unlike most Gila monsters, who did nothing ninety-five percent of the time, Gil did nothing ninety-nine percent of the time. With no one to fight and no opportunities to mate, his only tasks were foraging for food and water, both of which were plentiful in a territory as vast and varied as his. This morning, driven by boredom and an energy surplus other animals would kill for, he was arranging and rearranging the rocks at the entrance of his shelter.

He flicked his tongue. What's that? Someone approaching.

The olfactory molecules he brought back to the roof of his mouth told him it was a male. A potential rival. Gil poked his head out. The sun was shining, and the temperature was eighty-eight degrees. Ideal conditions for a wrestling match.

He went back and forth in his mind. Why bother if it always ended the same way? But he could use the practice in the event his lifelong social constraint, by some miracle, were to get resolved. He chewed a wad of fresh *Salvia columbaria*[1] leaves, a pile of which he kept on hand for times like this. Not that they'd ever made a difference.

---

1 desert chia

The fluorescence of the invader's pink-orange bands meant he couldn't have been more than three years old, and explained his presence—he was too young to know better. He'd think his youth and speed were enough to overcome Gil's experience, weight, and home-turf advantages. Under ordinary circumstances, he might have been right.

"*Qui va là?* (Who goes there?)" said Gil in a shout.

The young lizard came closer. "I am Marcel, and I am faster and stronger than you, *monsieur*. When I defeat you, what was yours will be mine."

They were always confident at the outset.

Gil turned his back. "I am ready!"

Marcel stopped. "You offer me the dorsal position *dès le début* (at the outset)? Are you mad?"

(Marcel's reaction was to be expected: bouts between Gila monsters typically featured a series of moves by both combatants—Head Nudge, Shove, Neck Arch, and Head Raise—before an aggressor attempted a Dorsal Straddle.)[2]

Gil shook his head, still facing away. "What are you waiting for? *Allons-y!* (Let's go!)"

"*Oui, monsieur.* It will be my pleasure." Marcel crawled on Gil's back and hooked his forearms under Gil's, ready for action.

After they alternated Tail Wraps, Gil walked in a small circle with Marcel clinging to him.

Marcel said, "Is that all you have, *pépère* (old man)? My great-grandmother could do better!"

Gil wasn't that old, only ten (middle-aged for a Gila monster), but he didn't argue. He kept his mouth fastened tight while performing a Neck Arch, which Marcel opposed with a Dorsal Head Pin.

---

2   These and other *Heloderma suspectum* wrestling maneuvers have been described by Demeter (1986) and Beck (1990).

Rachel Ivanyi

"Submit, *monsieur!*" said Marcel. "This is not a fair contest!"

Gil was irritated at the condescension. Why couldn't they have a gentlemanly duel? He initiated a Lateral Rocking, trying to separate himself, but Marcel held on and countered with a Tail Thrash.

Had Gil spoken, he'd have said, "*Pas mal* (Not bad)."

"Aha!" cried Marcel. "See how your ridiculous efforts are wasted."

Gil upped the ante with a Body Twist. Instead of getting free, he received a Shoulder Bite, which didn't break his bone-encrusted skin, but hurt. "Ow!" he said, before he could catch himself.

Marcel fell off in a fit of gagging. Thick tears streamed from his eyes as he scrambled backward. "Your breath, *monsieur...c'est...horrifique!*" He turned and ran.

Gil called after. "I'm sorry! Come back! I'll keep my mouth shut, I promise!"

His opponent disappeared behind a barrel cactus.

Gil was mad at himself. He should have let Marcel straddle him longer, just for the experience. Or the companionship, adversarial though it was.

One week later, Gil poked his head out and thought about rearranging the rocks again. He hadn't moved since the episode with Marcel.

He caught a whiff of reptile. *Quoi?* Back so soon?

No. This time his tongue told him it was a female.

A female! *Oh, mon Dieu* (Oh, my God).

He grabbed more of the minty leaves, grinding his teeth together like he was latched onto the leg of a murderous coyote.

She came into view from around the barrel cactus.

Gil stepped outside and spoke with his head turned away. "*Mademoiselle*, you must be lost!"

She kept coming, slow and steady. "I am not lost. I am Vivi. And you are Gil."

Gil was verging on panic. What to do? Where to go? He did nothing but chew (with his mouth closed).

Vivi stopped her advance on a large flat rock. "Do you mind if I lie here? *Le soleil est merveilleux* (The sun feels amazing)."

Gil finally faced her and nodded. His slow head movement was in sharp contrast to his tongue, which darted in and out like a crazed caterpillar. She smelled so sexy.

"You do mind then?" she said.

He shook his head no, quicker this time.

Vivi's tongue flicked too, and she caught a whiff of Gil's breath, from his nostrils. She stifled a sudden urge to vomit. "I found you," she said.

Gil was sure this must be some kind of cruel joke, played on him by Marcel or some other male who was envious of Gil's resources.

"Talk to me," said Vivi. "I can handle it." She flicked her tongue and stuck her neck out.

Gil stopped chewing. "You...know?"

Vivi couldn't help but turn her head in disgust. Gil was mortified. She spoke quickly. "*C'est bon je le promets* (It's fine, I promise)."

Gil didn't know how to respond.

She said, "*Je souffre* (I suffer from) the same *maladie* as you."

Gil flicked and flicked. What? The same...?

All he could smell was her delicious femininity and carrion, which she must have eaten recently, because she had pieces of it stuck in her teeth. (Gil loved carrion, especially dead birds, but stayed away from it for obvious reasons, though it wouldn't matter anyway.)

"And I've never mated," she said.

A virgin? (Like he was!) Talking to him? He thought he might pass out.

"I've never even been kissed," she said.

Gil stared, blinking and flicking.

She said, "Here, I'll show you." She crawled to within a body length (about two feet), opened her mouth, and exhaled straight at him. "See?"

Gil lapped it up, confused. There was nothing wrong with her breath. It was the most beautiful, perfect thing he'd ever experienced.

"I am very sorry to correct you, *mademoiselle*, but you are mistaken."

The olfactory fatigue she'd prayed for set in. She stepped past him and inside, by the pile of leaves. "Ooh, *mes préférées*! (my favorite!) Can I have some?"

"*Bien sûr, mademoiselle*, as much as you like."

She grabbed a mouthful and started chomping. Before Gil could help himself to more, Vivi's forked tongue shot forward, tickling his snout. He stood frozen.

She stopped chewing. "*Embrasse-moi* (Kiss me)," she said.

He let his tongue slither out. She wrapped hers around his and they looked into each other's eyes. The two fleshy black organs twirled, rose, and fell like *danseur* and *danseuse* performing a *pas de deux*.

Gil felt his two hemipenes poking out from under his belly. Vivi must have assumed as much, because she rotated her rear end until they were side by side, taking care not to disrupt their oral engagement. They closed their eyes. She lifted her tail. He put a leg on her back. She scooted in closer. He put the tip of one hemipenis into her cloaca. She quivered. It was the most amazing sensation he'd ever felt, and he climaxed within seconds. The hemipenis slipped out and right away he inserted the other one, this time deep into her vent.

Marcel was peeking around the barrel cactus at Vivi and the old man. *Révoltant*! How could she stand it? He was jealous too, knowing she'd be impregnated by the stinking *aristocrate*, but it was powerful leverage: if Vivi didn't behave, Marcel would use her maternal love against her before the children even hatched.

He waited five long minutes to make sure the couple were well into their lovemaking, and then it was time to act. He crept forward with his body low, his underside rubbing the smooth rock. He kept his tongue in his mouth, fearing if he picked up the scent of atrocious *exhalation*, he'd forget himself and alarm his target.

Vivi had done exactly as Marcel had asked, positioning the old man so the hind leg opposite her, the one on the ground, was facing out.

Bien, Vivi. *Très bien* (Good, Vivi. Very good).

Marcel held his breath, though the noises and visuals were sickening enough. He concentrated on the exposed back foot.

Closer, closer. Ignore the intertwining tongues.

Closer.

He edged to within an inch before he struck.

Gil's heel gave way to the crushing power of Marcel's jaws, rendering Gil's foot (and its clawed toes) useless.[3] Gil gave a violent shudder. Vivi's tongue unspun itself and snapped back inside her mouth. A split second later she'd detached herself completely with a Shove (one of the few wrestling moves employed by females).

She ran to Marcel, who'd retreated to the barrel cactus. "Well, well, *monsieur*!" he cried. "Now you see! All that was yours, *sera à moi*!"

Gil looked at his foot. It was twisted and bloody. When he tried to move, the pain made him shriek.

Marcel said, "Listen to him now, eh, *mon amour* (my love)?" He took a step toward Gil. "And what a lover she is, *non*?"

---

3 *Heloderma suspectum's* evolutionary solution to the need for dexterity had come with an inherent weakness: though still armored, the feet and toes were areas of relative vulnerability.

Gil's hemipenes were still erect and glistening. Enraged and desperate, he charged, until his ankle gave out and he slid to a stop, off-kilter like a table with one short leg. He hissed and spat, but they were too far away.

Marcel spoke in a low tone. "I will return, *monsieur*, to claim my prize. *À bientôt donc* (until then)." He led Vivi, who was crying, around the barrel cactus, and they were gone.

Gil dragged himself back to the shelter. He'd already made up his mind: he was going to use his bad breath to defend his territory (the home base at least) until he died of thirst, which would happen before winter unless he died from infection first.

He thought of Vivi and felt forgiveness. She wasn't evil. She'd been taken advantage of. He hoped she'd come back before he expired, so he could smell her one last time. He settled in a spot where he'd see her coming, and from which he could reach the pile of *Salvia columbaria*, just in case. ♦

CARLOS FROM MONTANA

They'd all known it was coming, because the slaughter happened every winter around the same time, when the days were shortest. Because of Carlos's friendship with the badger, he'd been able to hide out in her den. Hundreds of other coyotes hadn't been so lucky.

"How many this year?" said Connie.

"They don't have final numbers yet," said Carlos. "And I don't want to know."

Connie reached into the wall freezer and handed him what smelled like a prairie vole, one of his favorites.

"Here, dude." she said. "This'll make you feel better."

"No thanks. Not hungry."

"Okay. Do you mind if I...?"

"Not at all."

She sucked on the icy rodent.

"It's senseless," he said. "Murdered, just for doing their job."

"Mm-hm." At least she couldn't see the grief on his face.

"There are places, you know, where these...*killing contests*... aren't allowed."

"Mmm..." The treat came out of her mouth with a loud pop. "Really?"

"Like Arizona.[1] Maybe we could...I mean, if you..."

"Yeah, that's really *far*. I can see why it'd sound attractive on a day like today, but the trip would be way riskier than staying. For you, too."

He sighed. "I'm sure you're right."

"What about the chorus? You still want to do it, no?"

---

1 Arizona outlawed coyote (and all animal) killing contests in 2018.

"I bet they have good ones in Arizona."

"But aren't the Helena Howlers, like, the best? Anywhere?"

"They're amazing." He always perked up when talking about the group.

"And they'll have openings now," she said.

"For sure." He was somber again.

"Well, then, I guess they need you."

"I don't...I don't know."

"You can do it. In fact, you should. Seriously dude, they need you."

He was quiet. She waited.

"There *is* a piece I've been working on," he said.

"So..." The vole had thawed enough, and she took a bite.

He said, "What if I embarrass myself?"

"Ing moff..." She chewed and swallowed. (She'd been trying to break the habit of talking with her mouth full.) "I'm not letting you out of this."

Again he was quiet.

"You know how I can be," she said.

"I do."

"Good. When can you try out?" She took another bite.

"There'll be an open call in the next few days."

She limited herself to gestures and soft grunts until she'd cleared her mouth. "This is your big chance, dude. You should be more excited."

"It's hard to get excited right now."

She set down the food. "Okay, I want to hear it."

"What?"

"The song."

"Now?"

"Yes, now. Go."

"But it's not...I need more practice."

Rachel Ivanyi

"Whatever. Start."

"The acoustics aren't right in here."

"Uh-huh. I'm waiting." She tapped her long claws on the dirt.

"I haven't warmed up, plus..."

"Sing already!"

"Okay, okay."

He cleared his throat, inhaled, and began.

O give me a home where the house cats all roam

Where the birds and the cottontails play

It was shockingly loud. After the last chorus, he reopened his eyes to the pitch black.

Connie ignored the throbbing in her eardrums. "That was great!" she said.

"Really?"

"Yeah. Do it like that, you'll get in for sure."

"You're not just saying that?"

"Come on, you know me. Anyway, it's gonna be outdoors, right?"

It was Carlos's turn and he was very nervous. It didn't help that the two coyotes who preceded him were in a different league, talent-wise. Tone, pitch, dynamics—superior in every aspect, he was pretty sure. He thought about leaving, but what would he tell Connie?

(Speaking of, where is she? Must be here, but lying low. Doesn't want to pressure. Maybe she's running late, or maybe she was way early. She's capable of either.)

"Next!"

Carlos hesitated and looked around, hoping somebody would cut to the front of the line. Nope.

The coyote behind him, a tenor named Fred, gave a friendly nudge. "You're up, man. Good luck."

Carlos tried to thank him but nothing came out.

He stood in the center of a small clearing. The snow was packed, making it comfortable to stand or sit. The three coyotes who faced him looked like movie stars.

The middle one said, "I'm Clovis, and this is Belle." He pointed left. "We also have Joaquin." He pointed right.

Belle and Joaquin waved.

Carlos said, "I'm so sorry for your loss." His voice cracked, but at least he'd been able to speak.

"Thank you," said Clovis. "Life goes on for the living."

Joaquin said, "Amen."

"And thank you for coming," said Belle.

Carlos said, "I've been a huge fan for years. The way you..."

Clovis cut him off. "We certainly appreciate that. Please go ahead. Whenever you're ready."

Carlos nodded and took a last glance around for Connie. *Focus, dude*, she'd be saying.

And he did, singing his heart out.

The panel looked at one another, and when Carlos thought he couldn't take the silence any longer, Clovis spoke.

"You're not quite right for us at the moment, but we value your participation and talent, and wish you the best in your future singing endeavors."

Joaquin said, "Next!"

"Exit over here," said Belle. She pointed to a path.

Carlos was numb. All that practice, preparation, the *anxiety*, and for what? Rejection without a callback. He'd wasted his time and everyone else's. Including Connie's. Where was she, anyway?

The sun was going down. They could commiserate in the coziness of her den.

When she wasn't at home either, he started to worry. If she'd decided to skip the audition, she'd have just woken up to get ready for a night hunt. Had she already left? He went back out for a look around.

It was the smell that drew him. He recognized it right away, because of their first meeting, two years before. She'd made a stink, literally, believing he'd had bad intentions.

He found her lying next to a deer fence. The snow around and beneath her was stained red.

"Connie?"

She tried to lift her head but couldn't, because of the snare.

"Connie!"

"How was the audition? I would've been there, but as you can see..." She pulled and kicked, causing more blood to drip as the wire cut into the folds of skin on her neck. It was obvious she'd been struggling for some time.

He said, "Oh no! What...what can I do?" He put his face in close, to see if there was any way, any possible way, to release her.

"This thing? No big deal, don't worry about it. I'm just getting going. But tell me, did they hire you on the spot? I'm assuming you went through with it, because if you didn't..." She started to wheeze.

"Don't, okay...okay...I'll figure something out. You have to stay still, because the more you move..."

"I know how these things work, dude. I wasn't born yesterday. And, I was about to bag this nice fat pocket gopher for us to celebrate with." She coughed and kept coughing.

He waited for it to end. "To answer your question, *yes*, I'm in. They love me. It's a dream come true, and I couldn't have done it without you."

"That's cool, dude. Really." She paused. "Alright, I should get back to it."

"Don't do that, please."

"What are my choices?" She jerked violently against the snare, which didn't budge. She did it six more times. More coughing. She laid her head down.

He didn't know what to say. He licked the matted wound, tasting warm blood. Her breathing had become irregular.

She said, "I'll be in the front row. When is it again?"

"Shh," he said. "Let's lie here." He snuggled next to her, unable to hold back tears.

They heard the barking at the same time. It wasn't coyotes. Somebody was coming to check the snare.

Carlos stood, but Connie made no effort to move. She said, "Go on. I'll handle this."

He couldn't just leave her.

"I have them right where I want them," she said.

He whined.

"Get out of here. I mean it. You know how I can be."

The dogs were getting louder. Carlos saw a light moving erratically through the trees.

"I'll never forget you, Connie."

He ran back to her den. Even from there, under six feet of frozen soil, he heard the gunshot.

The walls reverberated with his wails, which nobody heard but him.

He wasn't hungry at all, but ate what was left in Connie's freezer: a bundle of earthworms, two mice, and a rabbit. He'd need all the energy he could get.

Creeping back out of the den, he sang to himself, quietly.

Where shelter abounds and friends gather around
Singing songs until night becomes day. ♦

THE SEVEN-LEGGED SPIDER

It was night.

"Hey McCooki! That time of year again, huh?"

"Yup! On my way to drop 'em off now. Wave everyone!"

Hi! the kids said in a chorus. They skittered all over McCooki's back and up and down her legs in a bulbous, rolling mass. McCooki was from the family Lycosidae—commonly called wolf spiders—the only spiders in the world who carry their live young.

"This is Gladys," McCooki said to her children. "She's a tortoise and a friend. She won't try to eat you."

She looks like you, Mama! With babies on her back!

"That's called a shell, and all tortoises have them. There's a story behind it, if you care to hear."

Yes, yes! Tell us the story of the shell!

"Yes, please," said Gladys. "I don't think I've heard it."

McCooki slowed to a stop. "You see, there once was a tortoise mother who was just like me, carrying all her babies on her back, everywhere she went. But they were naughty little tortoises and kept sneaking off to investigate things."

Investigate? That sounds fun!

"She finally told them: if you don't stay on my back, the chopper's going to get you."

Oh, Mama, what's the chopper? That sounds scary!

"The chopper is a monster that chops up naughty children."

Oh, no!

"Oh yes. And the next time those little tortoises slipped off their mother's back to go investigate something...the chopper caught them."

What did the chopper do?

"Chopped them up into little bloody pieces."

Oh, no!

"Oh yes. And when the mother tortoise found them, she was so sad, she put all those chopped-up pieces on her back, so she could keep carrying her babies everywhere she went. Eventually they turned hard, hard as stone, and that's how the tortoise got her shell."

Wow. Yay!

"Not sure about that one," said Gladys in a whisper.

"It's just a story," said McCooki, whispering too.

She heard the hoot of an owl. It wasn't near, but she ducked under the shadow of a leaf.

"You remember that sound, right, children? Not your friend. And see the moon? Don't travel if it's any bigger than this."

Okay, Mama!

The sudden light came from straight ahead. McCooki didn't move.

What is it, Mama?

"Okay kids, pay attention. These are called *people*. When you see one or more of them, don't run. Freeze. They're probably your friends."

What if they want to eat us?

"They don't."

The light is so bright!

"Yes, keep looking at it. That's how they see us. Because of our eyes that look like stars. Let them come right up to you. Keep staring. It makes them happy."

McCooki was glad for the opportunity to teach this lesson before the sendoff. (You never knew when people were going to appear. You could go years without seeing one, then for no apparent reason they come out six nights in a row. Then nothing again.)

This person walked straight at them. The light was trained like a spot.

It's scary, Mama!

"No, it's not, sweethearts. Stay on me, keep looking at the light, and everything will be glorious."

She felt pangs for Jesse and Trevor, whom she'd lost the year before, the only two out of ninety-seven. It hadn't involved a predator—some stones from the turrets around the edge of the burrow had fallen inside and on top of them—but it was just as painful for McCooki. And a reminder that she had to keep the kids on her back until the *last possible moment.*

She said, "You okay over there, Gladys?"

"Hell yes I am. Tell you what, the more these people see me, the more food shows up. How about you?"

"Good, good. It's a learning opportunity." She could feel the little ones crawling over and under one another. The light was brighter than day. "Keep looking, kids. It's okay. They're our friends."

But it's too bright!

McCooki asked Gladys to take over.

"I was gonna suggest that," said Gladys. She lifted a leg and cracked a stick with her beak, attracting the cone of white her way.

"Thanks, G," said McCooki. "See you later." She kept on, the same direction as before.

Mama! Tell us how the people got their light!

She already missed these kids, and they weren't even gone yet! So precious were the days—moments, really—she was given to spend with them.

"Well, for starters, people used to have more eyes, like us," she said.

"Really?"

Yep. And they could spin webs, too."

Wow!

"Uh-huh."

McCooki went on to tell her children, as they hung on in delight, how the people went to visit the Creator and asked for a swap: they would give up their web-spinning and most of their eyes in return for being taller.

No way!

"Oh yes. They left with only two eyes and no webs. But they had become very tall."

McCooki stopped moving, because they'd arrived at the launching spot. "People grew taller and taller, and their eyes were so high up they couldn't see what was in their way when they walked at night. So they reached up, because they were tall enough, and grabbed a piece of the sun and put it in a jar, to use whenever they needed.

Yay!

"We're here, so let's go through the big list one more time, alright? Things that want to eat us—yell until we have them all."

Coyote!   *Bobcat!*   *Raccoon!*

Mantis!   *Lizard!*   *Toad!*

Frog!   *Owl!*   *Woodpecker!*   *Bat!*

When one shouted *Salamander!* McCooki followed with "Excellent!"

The kids got them all, every possible predator, except for the wasps,[1] which McCooki hadn't told them about. (They'd either learn about the wasps or they wouldn't, just like they'd survive the education

---

1   not mud daubers; a different species of parasitic wasp

or they wouldn't. Knowing about the wasps now wasn't going to make the kids' life better. On the contrary.)

McCooki looked around but couldn't see much. Fine. It meant they couldn't be seen in return. As if they'd read her mind, the children asked for one last story.

"Which one?" she said.

A good one!

She suggested the story of how the wolf spider got its name, and they thought it sounded grand, until she said there was no such thing as a wolf.

Never?

"No, not never," said McCooki. "There used to be wolves, and they looked like coyotes, except they were bigger and faster and stronger and more terrible, far more terrible. But no longer, because the people killed them all. Because the people were afraid of the wolves and thought they were *too dangerous*.

The children were in awe of how dangerous something must be to make people want to get rid of it completely.

"That's right," said McCooki. "That's who you're named after, because you're scary!"

She shook in a way that let everyone know it was time to get off.

There was nothing she could have done. The coyote had spotted a few reflected glints of whatever light was coming from the sky when McCooki jostled her brood. Without knowing what it was, he pounced. (He could decide if it was edible after.)

A paw came down on McCooki.

(The coyote had the spider by its legs. Small but tasty. Good energy value. And crawling with newborns. Like a condiment.)

"Run! Now!" McCooki was yelling. The kids were yelling, too. She could feel the broken and smooshed spiderlings on her back and shoulders—felt each of them individually, she was sure. Some had gotten away, many had not, and a few clung to her still, because they hadn't been willing to let go.

"Go, all of you!" she screamed.

The children had never heard that tone of voice, and hurried to get down.

McCooki bit the coyote on the foot pad. Her fangs sliced through the layers of callous with ease, and though she might not have enough venom to harm something his size, it hurt, and he let up enough for Mc-Cooki to get three legs out. Now she was pinned by one leg only.

With the kids gone, she could turn her attention to getting away. Being a wolf spider, she could survive and overcome a missing limb (unlike other spider species). She twisted herself free, surprised at how little pain there was when the leg popped out of its socket. She skittered into a brush pile. She should scrape the flesh and blood of her dead children off her back, but she didn't want to. Not yet.

(The coyote ate the measly spider leg and left. Almost nothing was better than nothing, but disappointing too, after the encounter had begun with so much promise.)

McCooki saw one of her babies reaching the top of a blade of long grass. Was it Tyler? or Caleb? And a web balloon. Whoever it was, they were going to make it!

She felt a burning in her abdomen. Her legs buckled. She couldn't see what it was, because she couldn't move, because...it had to be a wasp. She was already paralyzed. That was the first part. Then she'd get filled with eggs that would hatch into baby wasps, who'd eat her alive from the inside out.

Her head was drooping, her thinking blurred. "Don't worry," she heard the wasp say. "Once the sting wears off, you'll feel surprisingly normal."

McCooki couldn't see the grass anymore, but imagined the tiny balloon had already carried her child off with the wind. ♦

PREY

Warner walked by two youngsters in the common area.

"I wanna be predator."

"No, I wanna be predator."

"You were predator last time."

"No, I wasn't. You were."

It had been only a few months since Warner and his buddies were that age and having that same argument, because nobody ever wanted to be prey.

He went past his burrow, then farther out, almost to the edge of the settlement. He was feeling good—strong, healthy, sleek—and the weather was the perfect mix of warmth and breeze for collecting seeds. He scanned the immediate area and, seeing no one, daydreamed and enjoyed the brightness of the sun for he didn't know how long.

When he saw the hawk, he turned and ran back to his burrow.

(Later he'd get asked: Why hadn't he seen the bird sooner? *Right over him*, it had flown.)

The hawk could easily have changed course. Sounding the alarm when he was supposed to would've been suicide.

He got to his hole and looked around. The bird had just passed overhead, diving at a shallow angle. Warner considered whistling but didn't, because it was too late. The hawk had already smashed into a squirrel with a loud thump and was flapping to regain altitude, pushing up pebbles and dust. It flew off, and Warner wondered which of his neighbors had been snatched (and if they were dead yet).

He did a slow three-sixty, scanning. To the west, directly behind him, he saw young Greta. Only her head was poking out.

How long had she been there?

If she'd seen the hawk, she'd have whistled. Or *should* have. It was everyone's duty to raise the alarm about approaching predators.

He decided she hadn't seen anything.

She crawled out, stood up, and pointed at him. Warner started to rise. "Yes?" He heard the screech of a far-off raptor and ducked. "Excuse? Me?"

Greta didn't say a thing or make any noise at all before disappearing into her burrow.

Warner went under too, and didn't come out until late the next morning.

Not knowing what to expect, and fearing the worst, he started with the top half of his eyes. Nothing.

Then his head. All clear.

He needed to get some food, after which he could come back and figure out what to do. He felt awful for whomever had been carried away by the hawk, but was he really expected to sacrifice himself for so-and-so because so-and-so wasn't looking?

He chose a seed patch that was a little out of the way and never crowded. A minute after he got there, another squirrel ran up.

"Hey there. Finally." It was Bernard (pronounced 'burr-nerd').

"Uh, me?"

"Yeah, you. I'm supposed to make sure you know about the emergency meeting. Dusk in the Galleria."

"Okay. Is there any reason...I...?" Warner wanted to know more, but wasn't sure how to ask.

"They want you there, is all I know. And I wouldn't mess with them if I were you."

Warner had another thought. "Do you know who got...taken?"

"You still haven't heard? It was Rodrigo."

"Oh. Rodrigo. Don't know him very well. Terrible, though."

"You *didn't* know him very well. He's gone now."

Bernard left. Warner had lost his appetite, but he forced himself against waves of worry to fill his cheeks for the storage bin.

He got back to his hole without seeing anyone else and stayed underground, pacing in tiny circles, for the rest of the day. The Galleria was at the opposite end of the settlement, so he left a little before sundown. On his way, he passed the spot where the hawk had struck. It took effort not to look for stray feathers from the collision.

Others were arriving, but avoiding him. Unless, of course, he was imagining all this, and in reality, everything was fine and normal. But everything couldn't be fine and normal, because if it were, there wouldn't be an emergency meeting.

What unfolded was Warner's worst-case scenario. The girl, Greta, with whom he thought he'd gotten along fairly well, accused him of "failure to advise of an incoming and imminent deadly threat." (Not her words, but an official summary of what she'd alleged.)

The entire assembly, sixty-two round-tailed ground squirrels (not including minors, who were in a side room, except for Greta), believed Greta's account before Warner had the opportunity to speak. When he did, it didn't help. What he'd thought was his best argument, "If she saw the hawk, why didn't *she* whistle?" came across as weak and evasive. This was about *his* duty, which he was now trying to pass off on a child. Had he no shame? They hurled scoldings and excoriations.

Then Warner tried to say he *had* whistled, but nobody had heard. Maybe his mouth had malfunctioned? He'd meant to whistle. Of course he had! It was instinct, was it not?

For a loyal squirrel, yes, was the response he walked right into, and they rejected his claim. His mouth hadn't stopped working at exactly the wrong time, they said. Those things didn't happen. And if his purported whistle had made a sound, any at all, someone would've heard, because it occupied a frequency squirrel ears had been hyperattuned to for millennia.

Warner was desperate. He was headed for banishment. He could feel it. He didn't know what else to try, so he tried reason.

"I don't know how the bird got so close, okay? But if I'd whistled when I saw it, I'd be dead! Okay? Dead! Is that my loyal obligation? To kill myself?"

There were shouts of "Moral duty!" but the chair regained control and explained: what was being deliberated in the present instance was civic duty, not moral duty.

Bernard stood. "Warner's a fine squirrel, what I know of him. But here's the problem, as I understand it. He ran to his hole before he whistled was what he did. And that's not the way it's supposed to work. We're supposed to whistle first, so everyone can make it to a hole."

Rodrigo's father cleared his throat and announced himself to scattered sniffles. "What happens if we all decide, from now on, when we see trouble coming, we're going to run to our holes before we sound the alarm? Is that what we're all agreeing to?"

The chair reminded the assembly that nobody was being asked to agree to anything with respect to alarm calls. They were there to discuss what to do with Warner. To figure out what punishment best served the group and best served the victim.

According to the letter of unwritten squirrel law, Warner should be banished. Over the years, these squirrels had put a significant allotment of their natural selective might into defensive alarm calling. They didn't have the hind legs of a kangaroo rat (which could spring nine feet in any direction), or the fangs or ferociousness of a grasshopper mouse, or the brains of a pack rat. The squirrels' chosen survival strategy was *cooperation*, and by remaining silent, Warner had violated their social contract.

Banishment. Warner knew it was coming. How could he have not seen that little girl in that hole? He should have checked, and kept checking, there and everywhere. So stupid! And now, he'd have no place to go, because no other colony would want him either.

They were getting ready to vote when Greta spoke. Her parents were as surprised as everyone else.

"Let him stay," she said. "Please. He didn't mean it. I don't want to be responsible for anything bad happening to him. Or anybody." She was crying.

Warner felt like he'd been pulled from the flames at the last possible moment. She was going to persuade them! As sure as he'd been that they were going to banish him, he was now sure they weren't.

They asked him to wait in the tunnel while they tallied.

He didn't get the final count, or who was for or against (although he could guess), but he was told he could stay, as long as he promised to never again run to his hole, or do anything else, before sounding an alarm.

Rodrigo's family and friends thought letting Warner off with no punishment was wrong for the colony and wrong for squirrels in general. They organized a strike for whenever Warner was above ground. (Meaning whenever he came up, they went below.) The strike caught on, not because there were so many squirrels with strong feelings, but because nobody wanted to be called a Warner apologist. Even Warner's immediate family, with whom he wasn't close and hadn't spoken to since the incident, joined in. It just seemed *easier*. For the time being.

Warner arrived at the rendezvous spot.

"You're late," said the hawk. A gust of wind ruffled the contour feathers on her head.

"I got held up, sorry. Need to be extra careful."

"What do you have for me this time?"

"I won't be able to stand lookout, obviously, but I can tell you they'll all come out tomorrow right before sundown. All of 'em together. And they'll be vulnerable in the transition."

"How do you know?"

"Because they won't come up while I'm there. Long story. Anyway, watch me. When I go in the hole, start your dive. By the time you get low you'll have your choice."

"Sounds like it could work."

"It will. But do me a favor. There's a young girl just west of me, moved in not too long ago. Please try and avoid her and her family, okay? If possible. Right next to me, west side."

"I'll do what I can." ♦

PREDATORS

The skunk shouldn't have been out during the day.[1]

Vance was only four. In his prime. Not old enough to be having eyesight issues. But after a few months in a row of unsuccessful hunting at night, he'd begun to struggle at dusk and dawn, too.

He could see fine in daylight, but because many bobcat prey aren't diurnal, there simply weren't enough chances. Vance was thin, hungry, and on the edge of panic. He needed to figure out some way to survive *without* being able to see in the dark.

The skunk was just standing there. Staring off into space, like it was daydreaming or having some kind of mild seizure, until it shook its head and kept walking, straight across a meadow of dark soil and patchy low grass with pebbles.

Out in the open, not a care in the world.

Vance figured there must be other predators watching, too. If he was interested, he'd better move fast. He looked up at the scattered trees. No raptors that he could see.

He knew something was off, but was too hungry to argue with himself. He needed a legitimate meal, something more than bugs and worms, so he could get his mind straight. He stalked the skunk from the left flank, keeping one eye on the sky.

As his prey neared a jojoba thicket, he pounced.

---

1 Skunks are nocturnal. Their distinct black-and-white warning coloration is a defense against predators with night vision. Prey animals use warning coloration to advise would-be predators of possible consequences. For example, "I taste horrible," or "I bite back," or "I can spray you in the face with something noxious."

Aware of the skunk's dangerous toxicity from behind, Vance stayed to the side, putting his jaws over the top of the small mammal's neck.

He clenched. This one didn't resist. That was odd too.

He didn't wait as long as usual to let go. He sat up to survey his kill.

In the time it took Vance to blink, the skunk had jumped in the air, twisted its body, and used its needle fangs to latch onto his cheek. Dangling, it clawed at his chest.

How was the crazed animal alive? The pain in Vance's face was distracting. And he was so hungry. He pinned the snarling devil against the ground and positioned his jaws around its throat again. This time he made sure there was a snap.

The skunk *should have* used its reprieve to spray Vance in the eyes. From point blank the effect would have been devastating, ensuring escape. But the skunk didn't do that; instead, it opted for close-range combat with a killing machine.

The only reasonable explanation Vance could come up with was the animal was not in its right mind. He decided to not think about it anymore. After eating he felt better, although his face still hurt.

A week later, Vance was on his way to a place with occasional water, hoping to find daytime prey. He passed a mesquite with large swaths clawed out of its bark. Paying attention to the smells, he realized he'd wandered to the border of a neighbor's territory. Her name was Wilma and she didn't like visitors, except when she wanted sex.

She had kittens now, he remembered. Or maybe not. Yes, she did. He could hear them! He stopped to listen.

"You be prey!"

"No, you be prey!"

"I don't wanna be prey! I was prey last time!"

"No, you weren't! I was!"

Normally it would have made Vance smile, but in his present condition, unable to feed himself, it made him sad. And angry. Having eaten almost nothing since the skunk, he was famished. He'd thought about moving closer to the city—if territory was even available—but had always decided not to, because he had no experience with people. Now, it seemed human garbage might be his only hope for avoiding death by starvation.

He narrowed his pupils and looked again. The markings he thought he'd seen on the tree were just sunburn. He sniffed, no longer detecting the odors of female urine and feces. Had he imagined them? He listened for the kittens.

Nothing. But they were just here!

Realizing he was still in the middle of his own territory and there was no way he could've heard any kittens, he became very confused.

It must be the lack of nourishment. He decided on the city. Staying was no longer an option. He hoped to find water along the way. Thirst had lately become an issue also.

Vance hadn't planned on fighting the woman. He was so hungry, that dog was exactly what he needed. If the woman had let go from the beginning, everything would've been fine.

She did let go when Vance scratched her neck. He took the dog back to the drainpipe, which was overgrown with sticky vines and a perfect place to hide.

The woman was dead before the ambulance arrived. There was nothing anyone could've done. A claw had opened her carotid artery.

Early the next morning, five bobcats met at the confluence of the Tanque Verde and Pantano Washes. Wilma was there, along with another of Vance's neighbors, Luther, and three cats from the city's edge.

Everybody—not just bobcats, but *everybody*—was talking about the attack on the human, and what was going to happen next.

Wilma's kittens lay at her feet, tired from the long early-morning walk. She said, "Won't he die from the infection soon?"

James said, "Probably, but we can't depend on it. We have to do something now."

Adia said, "For sure. We can't have a rabid bobcat going around killing people."

Before any of them were born there'd been an incident, part of local legend, in which a group of bobcats tried to euthanize a rabid neighbor. Others got infected, and in the end, four more died. It was agreed that if a like situation were to arise in the future, they'd solicit the help of their archrivals, the coyotes. (Asking the pumas would have been pointless—they didn't get involved in what they called "down-chain dramas.")

Luther said, "Coyotes are conniving, thieving sons of bitches. I say we don't."

Shauna said, "I agree with James and Adia. We have to do *something*. If it's the coyotes, so be it."

None of them wanted to point it out, but the line of demarcation was clear: the city bobcats wanted the coyotes involved, and the country bobcats didn't. After more discussion, Wilma changed her mind and sided with James, Adia, and Shauna. She didn't need a big, strong, violent cat roaming around in *or* out of town. Especially with the kittens.

Luther said, "What makes you think they'll want to help?"

Wilma said, "When the humans bring out the guns, the coyotes get it the worst. They don't want a rabid animal on the loose any more than we do."

Wilma volunteered to meet with the coyote emissary, an out-of-towner named Carlos who'd earned a reputation for being kind. ("Yeah, *right*," Luther said with a snort.) She left the kittens with Shauna.

(Wilma didn't like coyotes either. No bobcat did. Coyotes were physically inferior to bobcats in almost every way, yet it was coyotes who sometimes preyed on bobcats, through coordinated activity. In making up for their individual shortcomings, coyotes had become, some would argue, the most formidable predators of all.)

Carlos seemed as friendly as advertised. Wilma said, "So you're not from here?"

"Nope, Montana, near Helena. Been here two years."

She wondered if his big ears were a Montana thing generally, or if it was just him. She didn't ask.

He told her he'd been chosen as emissary precisely because he *wasn't* steeped in the longstanding local conflict.

She said, "There aren't tensions between bobs and coys in Montana?"

"We're competitive, sure, but not like here. The bitterness! I'd like to get your take, but later. We have other things to go over."

Wilma was surprised at the one-sidedness of the coyotes' offer, and Carlos himself looked uncomfortable as he was conveying it. The coyotes would take care of the bobcats' problem if the bobcats would leave the house cats—all of them—to the coyotes.

"Forever?" said Wilma.

"Well, nothing is forever. But, kinda, yeah. We want to manage the population ourselves. You know we'll do a stellar job, and it'll bring stability further down." (He was referring to rodents, birds, lizards, etc.)

"What about the raptors?"

"They don't take enough house cats to matter."

"I'll have to see what the others say. I understand, I think."

"And I understand how hard this must be for all of you."

This coyote was different, for sure.

She said, "I didn't know Vance well, but yes, it's very sad. I might've had kittens with him at some point."

She took the offer to the other bobcats, and they accepted. They didn't love house cat meat anyway. Sometimes there were just *so many.*

The coyotes already knew where Vance was hiding and went to work that evening. They hadn't been aware of his vision problem—nobody had—but found out when they lured him from the pipe and he wouldn't look at any one of them.

Did the bob even know he was surrounded? And the snarling didn't seem to be coming from him, but from the virus stuffing his membranes. Like it was desperate for a new host.

Vance was the thinnest he'd been, but was no longer hungry. Nor could he drink anything, because his throat wouldn't allow it. [2] All he wanted to do was maim and kill. When Carlos stepped in close, Vance saw him and lunged.

Carlos led Vance on a chase until another coyote took over. Then another. They ran Vance in an eighth-of-a-mile oval, switching off every lap, so while the coyotes stayed fresh, Vance got more and more tired.

His run slowed to a walk, then a stagger, then a wobble. When he finally collapsed on the sand, the coyotes stood around him. He needed to be put out of his misery. (A dangerous task, even in his weakened and exhausted state.)

While one coyote distracted him from the front, another darted in to bite his rump or hind leg. They were extremely careful to allow neither Vance's teeth nor his claws to come close. Everyone was afraid of the virus.

---

2 The other name for the rabies virus is *hydrophobia,* which means, literally, 'fear of water.' The sufferer is dying of thirst while unable to drink.

Dozens of punctures later, Vance had lost a pint of blood. His energy ebbed, and he stopped trying to swipe at his tormentors. When Carlos was sure Vance was weak enough, he asked Hugo, a huge coy with a bite like an anvil, to finish the job on Vance's neck.

They dragged the carcass to a road. It was the middle of the night, so there was no traffic. They stayed nearby to guard against theft by a carrion eater. Soon the humans would come, and the problem would be solved.

When Carlos met Wilma after, he swore they'd made it as painless as possible.

She wanted to believe him.

He said, "The others want to make sure your side intends to honor the agreement."

"We do, and we will." She didn't swear to it, because she couldn't.

"Let's stay in touch," he said, "You and me, okay? I'd like that. Maybe this is the start of something."

"Sure, okay," she said. "I'd like that too."

Wilma was in a surprisingly good mood as she headed back to her territory, kittens in tow. Attracted to a coyote? Who'd ever heard of such a thing?

Yet, she couldn't deny it. ♦

SOMEBODY'S WAY

The last time something like this happened, two were killed and seven were wounded. No motive was established, and the perpetrator was never caught.

Now it was three young children, ages eighteen, twenty-two, and twenty-five, hacked to ribbons in the middle of the night. Babies! At the southern boundary of the canyon proper, near where the humans launched their projectiles.[1]

Rowdy's predecessor, Handy Andy,[2] had taken an arms-off approach to human affairs. In Handy Andy's view, saguaros were revered and protected by most people, and these killing sprees, while appalling, were infrequent and random. Besides, the humans could clean up their own garbage.

Rowdy's own experience was that humans were anything *but* clean and *nothing* they did was random. He wouldn't—couldn't—stand by and allow such a heinous act to go unpunished.

If you take a walk in the desert, unless it's during or after a storm, you won't see water. But it's there! And more plentiful than you think, hiding in the saguaros—giant repositories of rain, collecting, storing, and sharing as they see fit.

---

1 Saguaros at the boundary of the golf course are sometimes struck by wayward balls, but instances are occasional and don't cause harm. The cacti think of the embedded studs as jewelry.
2 Anders the Crested Saguaro commanded the canyon saguaros from c. 1870 to 2017, when he chose Rowdy as his successor. He died of natural causes in 2018.

Saguaros are a *keystone species* because they provide so much for so many: shelter against heat, cold, and predation for local and seasonal birds (many others besides woodpeckers, whom we all agree are *the best* and *most important*); food for pollinators—bees, doves, hummingbirds—during the spring flowering; and fruit with enough moisture and nutrients for dozens of animal species to survive the month of June.[3]

A crime against a saguaro is a crime against the desert itself.

Speaking of, there's a news story from forty years ago, about a cactus up north who dropped an arm on a man, killing him. The saguaro, a youngish ninety-year-old named Wyatt, died from shotgun wounds in the exchange. As far as anyone knew, the instigator was just another drunken menace with more ammo than brains.

This latest tragedy, it seemed to Rowdy, was completely different.

The luxury hotel chain's only Southwestern US location had a hundred and twenty rooms, eighteen celebrity-designed golf holes, and enough land at the back of the thirteenth for a clubhouse/bar/restaurant/live music venue/dance club that would make its owners even richer.

The developer was kicking himself. Stupid little saguaros—if he'd dug them up himself and kept quiet, the a-holes at the County wouldn't have noticed. Instead, in the interest of *doing things right,* he'd hired a saguaro-moving specialist. The specialist, knowing juvenile saguaros had a special designation (even on private property) and not wanting to lose his license, filed for permission. When the permit was denied, the developer's dreams of Studio 54 in the Foothills were put on indefinite hold.

Rowdy was right. This wasn't random violence. Those three young saguaros had been in somebody's way.

---

3   Saguaros bear their red, seeded fruit during the year's hottest and driest period.

The developer reported the crime in the late morning, after the day's first foursome told the pro shop staff about the vandalized cacti on thirteen. Who in their right mind would do that? the golfers had asked.

The sheriff came out and interviewed the developer, who was, if not an automatic suspect, a person of interest. He'd been disrespectful and threatening in his communications with county personnel regarding the denied permit.

There was evidence that pointed to the developer, in the form of a machete.

The developer said someone must be trying to frame him.

Who would want to frame him? the sheriff wanted to know.

A disgruntled ex-partner. One who'd thought his buyout, forced but allowable under the terms of the partnership agreement *he'd signed*, had been confiscatory and one-sided.

(Each man considered his own role in the venture's success more important than the other's. Immeasurably more. *Without me*, each believed, the project wouldn't have happened at all.)

The sheriff went to the ex-partner's address down the street. (Like the developer, the ex-partner lived in the gated community attached to the resort.) A felling ax was found, the kind used for chopping down small trees. Other things, too, suggesting the ex-partner was, in fact, the culprit.

The developer, who set up the whole thing, would have gotten away with it, but for the woodpeckers.

This was the third instance of woodpecker habitats getting wrecked in two generations.[4] And those saguaro youths had held such promise! They wouldn't yet be livable for another six generations, but from then

---

4 Gila woodpeckers can live for ten years, so two generations = twenty years.

on, they'd have housed woodpecker descents[5] for up to ten more. The birds were apoplectic. There'd been way too much drama in that canyon over the years, and this was the last straw.

Those who slept nearest had been awakened by the sound, a deep *thock*. The second blow was drowned out by the howling of the set-up-on child, who was in turn drowned out by the Blaring in full.

Three woodpeckers braved the noise, trailing the ax man to his car. They followed him as he drove across town. They were going to figure out where he lived and who his abettors were, if any, before deciding how best to fuck up *his* life, if for no other reason than to make themselves feel better.

Bad luck, bad decision, wrong place/wrong time, whatever—the guy had no idea he was being tailed, or how much trouble he was in. They followed him for days, until he met with the developer late at night in the parking lot of a shuttered big-box store.

Now the woodpeckers had two places to direct their ire.

The bogus setup had been stupid: a machete, covered with saguaro pulp, left in plain sight on the developer's front porch. The sheriff saw through it right away, of course, because the vandal hadn't used a machete.

The ex-partner had motive: the unfair buyout. And because he lived alone (acrimonious divorce), and the assault had occurred in the middle of the night, he had no alibi. And then there was the felling ax.

He was arrested and accused. He hired counsel and posted bail. The gears of the criminal justice system began their slow turn. The sheriff continued to investigate, but with much less urgency than before.

---

5   A group of woodpeckers is called a *descent,* or, alternately, a *drummer.* (Yeah!)

Rowdy gave his orders to Chad, who screamed. "To the neighbors of the slain!"

They waited.

"Volunteer for a sacrifice!" said Chad.

They all shouted, "VOLUNTEER FOR A SACRIFICE!"

Two saguaros responded, almost in unison but not quite. "Volunteer!"

All were silent.

Chad yelled, "The eldest volunteer!"

"THE ELDEST VOLUNTEER!"

"Ready to serve, at your command!" said hundred-and-eighty-year-old Armando. Giving up one of his eight twisty arms wouldn't kill him but was indeed a sacrifice. Fewer arms meant fewer flowers and fruit, which meant fewer pollinators and seed spreaders.[6] Also, it was going to hurt, and he'd have to deal with the risks of fungal and bacterial infection, insect infestation, and a literal *host* of other issues.

Armando was ready. He understood the task. He started emitting short bursts of sound, making him easier to locate than if he were supplying an uninterrupted stream. Just Armie (as his friends called him), yelling solo, hoping the woodpeckers would notice.

They *did* notice and went searching, though it was enough to shake their eardrums. The lone Blarer was right by where the young cacti had been butchered. This saguaro was trying to tell them something!

Armie kept it up, and more woodpeckers came. A dozen, then two dozen, then four, from all over the canyon, to help decipher what this old cactus, in piercing chirps and booming grunts, was trying to say.

---

6 Saguaros don't care about the abundance or viability of their own offspring per se, except in so far as it assists the overall saguaro population, which they care about very much.

One named Kyle (the great grandson of another named Kyle, who'd famously faked a concussion) figured it out, and the woodpeckers got busy preparing one of Armie's arms.

The bulldozers showed up a month later. The developer had always been very hands-on when it came to construction. He especially loved walking his lots as they were transformed from raw, chaotic desert into clean, level, *buildable* real estate.

He was feeling especially lucky the day he found piles of coins— pennies, nickels, dimes, quarters (and a silver dollar!)—just beyond his now-immaculate parcel on the canyon (north) side. Next to a large saguaro.

He wondered what those woodpeckers were doing on that cactus arm. All that pecking. Right over him. More woodpeckers in one place than he'd ever seen. He'd get back to that in a minute, after he picked up the rest of this money. Amazing!

Armie's arm fell straight down. The four hundred pounds of mass accelerating at 32 feet per second per second[7] flattened the developer like a bug. (He'd been a coxswain at Yale.)

All charges were dropped against the ex-partner. Not because they didn't believe he'd done it, but because a conviction was unattainable without the testimony of the developer.

The hit man, who'd done the actual chopping, was frustrated. Something was up with his mail. Important things he'd been expecting—waiting for—hadn't arrived. He hated going to the post office, but now he had to, to file a complaint, because somebody was *stealing* his mail. Maybe even his postman, who'd acted way too defensive when questioned. (It was the first time they'd ever spoken.)

---

7   acceleration due to earth's gravity

The left turn into the post office on River Road was dangerous. Because the road curved, you couldn't see quite as far as you'd like before having to cut across two oncoming lanes.

The birds blocked his view as he was inching out. He hesitated, then started the turn.

Now he was committed. But he couldn't see because of the birds. What the hell were they doing? He spun the wheel and floored the gas pedal. A pickup truck slammed into his Accord at fifty-five miles per hour.

The saguaros didn't know about the axer's demise, but it didn't matter. They knew they'd helped the woodpeckers get the developer, so they (and Rowdy in particular) were satisfied justice had been served, southwest desert style.

Rowdy told them all to let loose, gossip a little, yell at one another. Just for the joy of it.

Even Jeremiah was in a good mood, his still-impressive voice booming above the rest. The last time they'd had this much fun was when those pigeons covered the canyon in guano. The moisture, the shade, the fertilizer! Weeks of gooey debauchery were followed by a whole new crop of vegetation, including young saguaros *all over the place*. (The woodpeckers had suffered terribly from the shitstorm, yes, but they'd come back stronger than ever, to no one's surprise.)

That was before the humans had decided to extend their footprint toward the canyon.

Those were the days, thought Rowdy. And they'll be here again.

"Mister Rowdy," said Chad.

"Yes."

"It's time for the weather check."

The sun was at zenith.

"So it is," said Rowdy. "Go ahead."

Chad screamed. "Weather check!"

"WEATHER CHECK!" ♦

VIPERS

"Piper! Go!"

Jake was thrashing, flexing every muscle, but the tongs were too tight. He and his sister had been enjoying an early spring nap on the back porch when the strange men in uniform snuck up from the side of the house.

"I'm not leaving you!" she said.

"Please, Pipe!"

The lid slammed shut, putting Jake in blackness. He heard Piper rattling and hissing viciously until another slam was followed by silence.

"Are you okay?" he said.

"Yes, I'm right here. They got me."

Jake was upset. While Piper could and should have escaped, he'd blame himself if anything bad happened to her.

After a bumpy and disorienting car ride, the snakes were lugged in their containers for what seemed (to them) like a long way. Finally, they were dumped next to each other in a dry riverbed. The men backed away before turning and trotting off.

Once Jake saw Piper was alright, he let his frustration out. "Why, Pipe? You promised, if things ever got..."

"I *told* you not to trust him."

She was wrong, but it wasn't worth debating. He needed to figure out what the heck had happened. He suspected it had to do with the new lady who'd been coming around, sometimes when the man wasn't home. The way she looked at them and kept her distance, it was obvious she didn't like sharing a porch with rattlesnakes. He'd never convince Piper, though—to her, all humans were alike. Getting her to drink the man's water and help with the pack rats had been hard enough.

Thinking about the rats upset Jake even more—how they must've cheered and cussed and waved their filthy paws as he and Piper were carted away. "The man's going to be in trouble without us," he said.

"No, he won't. He'll be fine. One of our cousins will take over."

She hadn't intended it, but her comment hit Jake hard. He'd risked his life and gone against his own kin in order to cultivate the relationship—the first of its kind—and now someone else was going to slink in? No. No! It wasn't right. And anyway, it would never work.

"We have to go back," he said.

"Can we at least find somewhere safe to talk about it?" Piper raised her head. "We don't know what's out here."

"That's why I'm going up this tree."

"Come on, Jake! Let's find a hole *first*."

He thought getting a better read on the situation was the surest way to ease her mind. "Stay here. When I get down, we'll find a place to hide and come up with a plan."

He didn't wait for her to respond.

Resting on a branch eight feet up, he swiveled his head all the way around. He was observing, smelling, and heat sensing, using everything in his phylogenetic toolbox to try and determine where they'd come from. He saw a familiar outline: the mountains that dominated the sky on one side of the man's yard. Yes! Jake narrowed his search, looking for the telltale shape of the man's roof. Was that...? It might be!

He was about to crawl higher when he froze.

"Piper! Watch out!"

Piper smelled it too, and panicked. No hole was going to save her from a kingsnake.

Jake saw it in a patch of desert broom, slithering toward her.

"Don't move!" he said. They had the advantage if Piper stayed put.

She didn't, sprinting away from the scent. The kingsnake sped after her.

There was no time to think, and Jake landed with a thud between them. His sudden appearance stopped the predator's advance.

"Piper, get back here!"

She turned to see her brother staring down the black-and-yellow assassin.

"I'm coming!" she said.

The kingsnake was immune to the venom, but not the fangs, and two vipers were one too many. It retreated.

"See?" said Piper. "We're already in danger." She flicked her tongue in a nervous cadence. "What if it comes back?"

"It won't."

"But what if it does? What will we do?"

Not worried, Jake fibbed a little. "All the more reason for us to get out of here."

Piper was scanning the landscape, still on edge.

Jake said, "We're going to find a hole, like you wanted. You'll be safe there."

"*I'll* be...?"

"Yes, and I'm pretty sure I can get us home. I just need to check the route tonight."

Piper was silent. Jake was going to do what Jake was going to do. As usual.

They found a suitable burrow nearby. When night came, Jake peered out. The stars corroborated his earlier assessment, and he brimmed with optimism. He gave his sister a loving stroke. "This is gonna work, Pipe, I know it."

"When will you be back?"

"By dawn at the latest. And if I'm not...you know what? Forget that. I'll be back, *no matter what.*"

"Swear to God?"

"Swear to God."

He left, heading north by northwest.

At the bank of the riverbed, he crawled up and out, then across a wide expanse of cactus and creosote bush. He moved quickly and quietly, keeping one eye on the stars and the other on the desert ahead. He had no interest in food. All he cared about was finding the way.

Three hours (and a close call with a great horned owl) later, he saw lights—like the ones that let him know when the man was coming and going in the dark. He also knew what could happen if he got too close.

Should he turn back now and leave the rest for the following night, with Piper? No. It was too perilous. He needed to be sure.

It took another half-hour to reach where the lights were whizzing past in both directions, accompanied by unholy smells and sounds. He watched and counted until he'd identified a recurring window at what seemed like a regular interval.

He was halfway across when a single light came into view. He had no way of knowing the motorcycle was speeding.

He was two undulations from the dirt when he realized he wasn't going to make it. He said a prayer for himself and for Piper and for the man.

The rider slowed but didn't swerve.

Searing pain accompanied a crushing weight, and Jake knew he'd been run over. He kept on anyway, dragging the last quarter of his broken body like a sack of dead mice.

Piper heard a familiar voice at sunup. The man? Here? She'd promised she wouldn't go anywhere until Jake returned. But he hadn't, against *his* promise, and she'd spent the final hours of darkness fearing the worst. Now it was morning, and still no Jake, and...

Was it really the man? Why?

She poked her head out. It *was*! And he wasn't alone. She recognized the others as the same two who'd captured her and Jake the day before. Why were the three of them together? Her mind raced. Every instinct told her to stay hidden, but she couldn't help thinking: what would Jake do?

Lost and alone, she had nothing to lose. She came out all the way and rattled. When she was sure the man had seen her, she imitated Jake by silencing her tail and moving her head in small circles.

The man approached, slowly. They maintained eye contact as he crouched at a safe distance.

The other two men were jumping up and down as if *they* were going to get bitten, but the man acted like he didn't care and didn't even hear. He moved his own head in circles, in a way that would've made Piper laugh had she not been so scared.

The man stood up, and Piper did the only thing she could think of: she went where Jake had gone. The man followed her across and out of the wash and through the desert. She was going as fast as she could over the rough terrain. The man ran out wide and in front of her, holding the same tool the others had used before. He set it on the ground and moved his head in circles.

She was terrified but knew what to do. She positioned the center of her body in the grabber section of the tool. He lifted her gently and carried her in the same direction she'd been headed, only now they were moving much faster.

The man walked around cactuses and bushes and took a long detour to get past a fence, but Piper could tell they were going in a straight line overall. She felt hope creep in. Were they on their way home? Would

Jake be there? Maybe he'd already been rescued! She closed her eyes and prayed.

Traversing a noisy span, the man walked faster. She opened her eyes and recognized a tree, then a saguaro. When the smells became familiar, she knew. The man had saved her! Now, where was Jake?

They saw him at the same time, laid out on the porch. His back end was pointing off at an improbable angle, and he looked dead. No! Unthinking, she opened her mouth to wail. The man jerked in surprise, but didn't drop her. He set her on the bricks next to Jake.

Jake was still breathing!

"Oh, there you are," he said. "What took you so long?" His voice was so weak she could hardly hear.

"You swore," she said. She looked at his bent form. Something must have fallen on him, like a log or a boulder. With a cracked spine, death was certain. (It was only a matter of time.)

She prayed for a miracle, and he spoke again. "And as soon as I get better, I'll come for you. I mean..." His voice trailed off.

The man had gone to the house and returned with a large cloth. He set Jake on top of it and carried him to the garage. When Piper saw the man leave, followed by the other men, she remembered the noise and realized what must've happened. Jake had been run over.

Hope evaporated. Her little brother was gone for good, and she hadn't said goodbye.

She asked God if she shouldn't just die, too.

A month later, the man set out the morning water like always, but this time he left the door open, and she saw what looked like...smelled like...it was! Omigod omigod omigod! Jake!

The man stood aside and Piper went in to her brother. After a joyous and tearful reunion, she looked around. "So...*this* is how they live."

"It's the best," said Jake. "Always the right temperature, plenty of food, and no predators. None. Even the mean lady's gone—or at least, I haven't seen her."

Piper had so many questions—how long had he been back, what was that thing on his tail, how did he eat—and he answered every one with the carefree manner she'd grown to adore. He might look a little different, but he was the same Jake. Thanks be to God! (And, she couldn't deny, to the man.)

Jake explained how the man put down two bowls every day: one with water, and another with a hearty porridge that tasted like dove eggs and toads and squirrels. He pointed his snout at the sticks attached to his hind end. "I'll probably have to wear this stupid thing forever, meaning my exterminator days are over. But the pack rats aren't going to rest, and neither can you. Think you're up for it?"

"Well, yes..." She stuck her tongue out and winked. "And pretty soon I'll have plenty of help."

"Wait, you mean..."

"Only thirty-two more days." She rolled over and showed him the bump.

"Pipe! I had no idea!"

"I don't tell you *everything*, little bro."

"Awesome," he said. "Just awesome."

She'd never seen him so happy. ♦

THE END[1]

---

1   for now

THE APPENDIX

A View from Below

- Pack rats have shown resistance to Western diamondback venom, and Jake likely wouldn't be able to produce enough to kill an adult rat per day. However, with a clever combination of venom, puncture wounds, head trauma, and constriction, he could do it. He'd have to be committed, which he is.
- Pack rats don't actually live in garages, but they love to loiter there while urinating and defecating.
- Snakes don't have eardrums. They detect sound waves with their jawbone and, to a lesser degree, with their lung.
- There is no clear understanding of what happens when one Western diamondback bites another. Because their venom is stored in enclosed sacs and doesn't come into contact with their own bloodstream, they may be able to envenomate themselves!

Casey and Calypsa

- Most black widow spiders have poor eyesight.
- As far as we know, the hourglass marking on black widows has nothing to do with sex or mate selection. The prevailing theory is the hourglass is *warning coloration* for repelling would-be predators, such as birds. It doesn't work against praying mantises, which don't see color and wouldn't care anyway.
- A female black widow has never been observed eating her mate in the wild. Her name and reputation seem undeserved. Please remember: Calypsa eats neither Casey nor Rick nor Tim.

- While female black widows can live for years, males live for only a few months.

Hum, Hum, Hum
- A praying mantis probably couldn't eat a whole hummingbird in a single meal.
- Montana coyotes don't really have larger ears than Arizona coyotes. They don't sing better, either.
- This is the first of eight stories in which coyotes appear—the most of any species, with one exception (and it's not woodpeckers).

Rarebit
- Unlike rabbits, who are born hairless and helpless, hares are born furred, eyes open, and ready to rock.
- Lazarus is a black-tailed jackrabbit, slightly smaller than the other species common to Southern Arizona, the antelope jackrabbit.
- Jackrabbits are the only mammal known to eat creosote leaves, and only as a last resort. While Thaddeus could eat creosote in real life, he'd be unlikely to find it "delicious."
- The following words, not found in *Watership Down,* are my own additions to the Lapine language: *lagilf* (hare), *lagytle* (rabbit), *toncinga* (poison), *lagomy* (rabbit or hare), *mesta* (lover), *cadú* (tail), *ternessi* (sentinel).

Still Standing
- It has been theorized by me (and others, I assume) that saguaros have a better understanding of weather patterns than we do.

- Crested or *cristate* saguaros are rare. Estimates range from one in fifty thousand to one in two hundred thousand.
- It's unlikely you could pile enough bird poop on a saguaro arm to make it fall off. Maybe if you did it in stages—let dry, re-coat, repeat.

Sarina's Descent

- Gila woodpeckers build homes in saguaros *and* mesquite and other hardwood trees. They seem to prefer saguaros, but we're not sure why.
- Both Gila woodpeckers and mourning doves mate for life.
- It's unlikely that a woodpecker boot would be large enough to accommodate some of the action portrayed. Also, I don't know if Gila woodpeckers can fly as high as a thousand feet above the ground.
- A cloaca in most birds (female *and* male) has three functions: urinary, excretory, and reproductive. I emphasize that most male birds *do not* have a penis.
- It might be true that pigeons prefer to poop while sitting or standing. One theory for this: if they poop in flight, they risk soiling their own feet. Okay! And, it seems to me they can poop whenever and wherever they want.

Wolf!

- If a pack of wolves kills an entire population of sheep, that's an *extirpation* event; not, as Lorna believes, an *extinction* event, which would wipe out the entire species worldwide. (To Lorna, it would feel like the same thing.)
- Bighorns are highly susceptible to diseases carried by domesticated livestock, especially sheep and goats.

- Mountain lions who kill bighorns have been tracked and killed by humans in order to help translocated sheep populations take hold.

Metamorphosis

- Schooling behavior in spadefoot tadpoles has not been observed. But why not? Even though these tiny swimmers are just a larval stage, they *do* have a lateral line, the same nervous system equipment fish use for schooling.
- When spadefoot tadpoles are metamorphosizing in a rapidly disappearing puddle, a small percentage of them will grow teeth, turn carnivorous, eat other tadpoles, and reach their adult form much faster than normal—so they can hop away before the water evaporates. This is an example of environmental gene expression.
- Male spadefoots, like male woodpeckers (and most other birds and amphibians), release sperm from a cloaca. They do not have a penis.
- You can see the spades in Rachel's illustration: Look for the black "spot" on the inner side of each heel.

The Neotenic Queen

- Research has shown that, among subterranean termites, neotenic queens are born through parthenogenesis and not sexual reproduction. In other words, neotenic queens are exact genetic copies of their mothers, in order to avoid the possibility of a king fertilizing the eggs of his own offspring. (Matsuura 2017)
- Termite kings and queens use pheromones and feeding programs to control the activities and destinies of their children, i.e., every member of the colony.

- In case anyone's confused, that big cream-colored thing on the cover is *Mother's belly.*

The Stigma
- There are a few other species of birds besides *Phainopepla nitens* that eat desert mistletoe berries on occasion. The berries are edible for humans, but require lots of preparation.
- Individual mistletoe plants are either male or female.

Alien Space Bats
- White-nose syndrome (WNS) is a fungal infection wiping out huge numbers of bats worldwide, including, according to some reports, free-tailed species, which until recently had been considered immune (for reasons unknown).
- Almost all bats have tails. When Liz refers to her "tailless cousins," she's talking about non-free-tailed species, whose tails don't extend past the webbing between their hind legs.

The Fall of Jericho
- Mountain lions will eat hares in the wild, given the opportunity. Taste isn't so important when you're starving half the time.

Reds
- Thanks to Ray Schweinsburg for writing such a thorough and amazing dissertation (Schweinsburg 1969) on these remarkable animals.
- When mine shafts were being dug in the mid-1900s in the Tucson Mountains, sometimes a crew would begin and then for any of number of reasons have to move over and start again.

This is how the unfinished shaft that eventually buried Boris and Katya came to be.

- The names of Carmine's crew—the Pigs to the North—are all shades of red.
- Peccaries who are unable to graze enough due to illness, old age, or injury are left behind and will starve or get eaten by predators.
- Not long after Rufus left, Katya figured out how to collect and store rainwater, and the Pigs (who aren't pigs) *really* had it made.

French Kissing for Beginners

- The Shoulder Bite is not an officially recognized Gila monster wrestling maneuver.
- The mythology of Gila halitosis runs deep: nineteenth-century scientists believed these lizards could knock prey unconscious just by breathing on them.
- David Brown (in the preface to Brown and Carmony 1999) describes an encounter with a three-legged Gila monster who appears to be thriving. It is my sincere hope that I was wrong about Gil, and he goes on to suck face (*sucer la poire*) and lay pipe (*s'envoyer en l'air*) like a champ for another decade.
- Demeter (1986) described a Gila monster biting another Gila monster on the leg with "no apparent provocation."

Carlos From Montana

- Usually, a badger den would be too small for a coyote to wriggle into. Connie had made hers larger to accommodate her friend.

- Carlos has big ears relative to most coyotes because his parents had big ears. As to why his big ears don't make him a better singer, I can't say.
- Coyotes and badgers are known to hunt together, but they don't share their kills.

The Seven-Legged Spider

- If you've never gone out at night in the summertime and looked for wolf spiders with an LED flashlight by your temple, do it.
- *Schizocosa* (genus) *mccooki* (species), of the family Lycosidae (wolf spiders), is not as common in Southern Arizona as *Hogna carolinensis*, another wolf spider. But she had to be McCooki.
- Henry C. McCook studied ants and spiders. He did lots of other things, too.
- Like all spiders, including black widows, wolf spiders don't have ears. They "hear" by sensing vibrations.
- It's very unlikely McCooki's children would encounter a salamander in Tucson, but if they did, the salamander would want to eat them.

Prey

- The hawk probably plucked Rodrigo from the ground, but I wanted there to be a collision. Collisions do happen sometimes.

Predators

- Consider the legendary warning coloration of skunks. Wouldn't they be much harder to see at night, and thus catch, if they were all black? One would think so, but apparently not; the striped ones seem to be doing fine.

- Although rabies is not carried in the bloodstream, biting Vance *did* carry a small amount of risk for the coyotes. They could have gotten infected from fresh—but not dried—saliva on Vance's coat.

Somebody's Way

- But how can I write two stories about saguaro cacti and not mention buffelgrass? I didn't want the buffelgrass issue to crowd out everything else. (And buffelgrass does get a passing mention in "Rarebit.")
- Buffelgrass, an invasive species, was introduced to North America by US federal officials sometime before 1940. This was *not random*, but it did create a huge mess, which has *not been cleaned up.* (Rowdy was right on both counts.)

Vipers

- Like other reptiles, rattlesnakes don't produce external tears. They cry on the inside.
- This story marks the twelfth appearance of humans in this collection, well over even the eight appearances of coyotes, who in my mind are everywhere, always.

INDEX OF ILLUSTRATIONS

Original illustrations are watercolor on
300 lb. board-mounted watercolor paper.

BIBLIOGRAPHY

Adams, Richard (1972). *Watership Down*. London: Rex Collings.

Arizona-Sonora Desert Museum, 2021 North Kinney Road, Tucson, Arizona, 85743. www.desertmuseum.org

Beck, D. D. 1990. "Ecology and Behavior of the Gila Monster in Southwestern Utah." *Journal of Herpetology* 24, no. 1: 54–68.

Brown, D. E., and N. B. Carmony 1999. *Gila Monster: Facts and Folklore of America's Aztec Lizard*. Salt Lake City: University of Utah Press.

Demeter, B. J. 1986. "Combat Behavior in the Gila Monster (*Heloderma suspectum cinctum*)." *Herpetological Review* 17, no. 1: 9–11.

Matsuura, K. 2017. "Evolution of the Asexual Queen Succession System and Its Underlying Mechanisms in Termites." *Journal of Experimental Biology* 220, no. 1: 63–72.

Schweinsburg, R. E. 1969. "Social Behavior of the Collared Peccary (*Pecari tajacu*) in the Tucson Mountains." PhD diss., Graduate College of the University of Arizona.

ACKNOWLEDGMENTS

I'm grateful for every person on this list.

Rebecca Salome, my writing coach and editor
Frances Bowles, copy editor

Consultants

Craig Ivanyi, Executive Director, and Staff of the Arizona-Sonora Desert Museum

Rachel Ivanyi

Dr. Kevin E. Bonine

Dr. Victoria Canelos

Jennifer Pressler (rabbits, hares)

Dr. Raymond E. Schweinsburg (collared peccaries)

Professors Mary Shaw and François Cornilliat (French language)

Dr. Theresa Levy (French language)

Beta Readers

Dr. Michael T. Borchers, Dimo Canelos, Sylvia Canelos, Frank Franklin, Zanley Galton, Arianna Gray, Cindy Johnson, Adam Levy, Matthew Meyer, Tami Meyer, Janelle Moss, Aimee Nadler, Eitamar Nadler, Eric Nadler, Rudy Nadler, Matthew Staples, Morgan Staples, J. Fife Symington IV, Tara Turner

Others who provided feedback, help, and support

Liz Baker, Derek Bambauer, Emily Bauer, Regina Buckley, Allegra Canelos, Esme Canelos, Gregorio Canelos, Tommy Caplan, Homero Ceron, Jay Colasanti, Eric Collignon, Chris Conner, Roni Devorah, John Dowling, John H. Finley IV, Eric Harper, Noah Horton, Jordan Ivanyi, Lance Jungmeyer, Andrew Killom, Melissa Lal, Barbara Lett, Jennifer Lindquist, Jørn Maarup, David Marcy, Marie McGhee, Megan McPherson, Henry Meyer, Allison Moore, Teresa Nowak, Crystal Richt, Joe Rosenbaum, Heb Ryan, Bobby Sain, Barbara Sattler, Tim Schaffner, Robert Shaw, Thomas Shaw, Victoria Shaw (Hi Mom!), Robert Shuler, Efrem Sigel, Jonathan Sigel, Wally Smith, Annabel Symington, Marci Symington, Don Tringali, Pete Turner, Doug Woolsey

Special thanks to:

Matthew Staples and Dawn McMillan for bringing my characters to life in the audiobook.

Mike Levy at 11:11 Studios for the engineering, mixing, and co-production of the audiobook.

Tyler J. Meier for invaluable advice and encouragement.

Dr. Michael T. Borchers for suggesting a map.

Rachel and Gaby for their talent, skill, and creativity.

My wife, Sylvia, and my daughters, Esme and Allegra, for love and patience.

ABOUT THE AUTHOR
AND ILLUSTRATOR

Alejandro Canelos was born in Nogales, Sonora and raised in Tucson. He earned a BA in Biology from Harvard in 1992. His second story collection, *Hunters and Thieves* (Neotenic), was published in early 2023. In his spare time, he plays drums professionally—freelance, all styles—and sings tenor II in two community choirs. He enjoys hiking, mountain biking, cheering on the UA Wildcats, jazz, and spending time with his family.

Rachel Ivanyi is one of those strange people who like the smell of formaldehyde. It takes her back to the early days of working in a museum lab. She is at home among the preserved and mounted critters. She applies both her scientific and artistic training, giving animals everlasting life through art and bringing attention to environmental issues. Rachel received a BS in Zoology from U.C. Davis and Graduate Certification in Natural Science Illustration from U.C. Santa Cruz. Many of her paintings have been exhibited across the U.S. and internationally and are part of permanent collections, both public and private. Her illustration clients include *National Geographic, Scientific American,* and nature institutions around the world. Having taught a wide variety of nature art classes over the course of her 25+ year career, she is currently a core instructor for the Arizona-Sonora Desert Museum Art Institute. When she's not in her art studio, you will likely find her looking for reptiles, dancing, or hanging with her family.

Made in the USA
Middletown, DE
28 April 2023

29313386R00149